MONSTERS & VAMPIRES

The Movie Treasury
MONSTERS & VAMPIRES

Alan Frank

octopus

First published 1976 by
Octopus Books Limited
59 Grosvenor Street, London W1

ISBN 7064 05250

Produced by Mandarin Publishers Limited
22A Westlands Road, Quarry Bay, Hong Kong

Printed in Hong Kong

CONTENTS

NOTE The dates of films given throughout this book are approximate. This is because of varying lengths of production-period, the intervals between production and distribution and differing dates of distribution in various territories. In most cases the date given is the year of principal production.

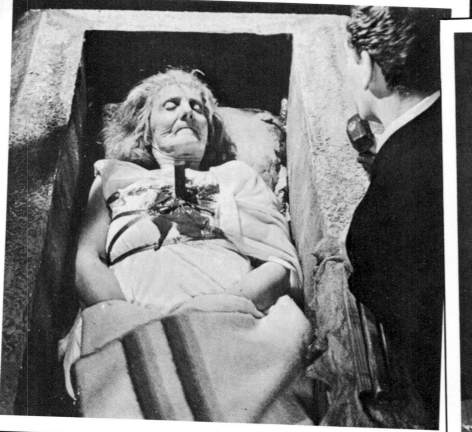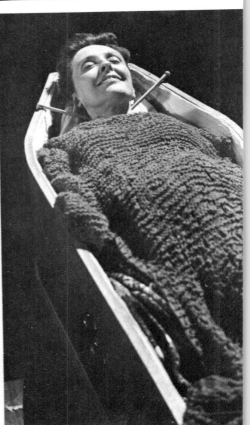

THE FIRST VAN

Long before Bram Stoker published *Dracula*, Vampires abounded in "real life", legend and literature. The concept of blood as a life source was prevalent in many and disparate cultures, from Leviticus in the Bible, which speaks of "The life of the flesh . . . is in the blood", to ancient civilizations in Central and South America, Babylon, Egypt, Africa, Assyria, Northern Europe, Greece and in the Roman Empire.

In real life there was Countess Elisabeth Batory of Transylvania – the inspiration for Hammer Films' *Countess Dracula*, an all too human monster who killed over 600 young girls and drank their blood. Gilles de Rais, too, was a blood drinker, while in more modern times the one-time director of London's Onslow Park Hotel, John George Haigh, was hanged on August 15, 1949, for murdering his victims, then opening their jugular veins and drinking their blood, before disposing of their corpses in a bath of sulphuric acid.

In literature, many Vampires preceded Stoker's Count Dracula. Goethe wrote of the Vampire in *Die Braut von Korinth*. Two of the group who wrote horror stories along with Mary Shelley, author of *Frankenstein* – Lord Byron and Dr. John Polidori – wrote novels of the Vampire.

Sheridan Le Fanu wrote *Carmilla*, while other Vampire short stories such as Marion Crawford's *For the Blood is The Life* and *Four Wooden Stakes* by Victor Roman kept the blood flowing. In 1847, Thomas Prest's *Varney The Vampire* appeared and then, in 1897, Lord Ruthven was supplanted, forever, by Count Dracula. Bram Stoker, who for 27 years was the actor Sir Henry Irving's business manager, supposedly wrote *Dracula* after a nightmare about Vampires brought on by "a too generous helping of dressed crab at supper one night"!

Christopher Lee, no mean expert on Bram Stoker and the origins of the Vampire in legend, literature and life, has no doubt that Stoker found the name of his creation from history. Says Lee: "Obviously he (Stoker) didn't invent the name. He must have found it somewhere. Vlad the Fifth at the end of the 15th century was Prince of the State of Wallachia, part of what is known as Transylvania. He was, in his lifetime, one of those rare beings – a real monster. He was a brilliant general, a tyrant, a genuine sadist and a frightening, ferocious and terrifying man. His battles against the invading Turks, during which he impaled some 10,000 Turkish prisoners, earned for him the name of Vlad the Impaler."

MPIRES

Below left. *Max Schreck as Graf Orlok, the screen's most repulsive Vampire in* Nosferatu *(Prana 1922)*

Below right. *Shadow of Evil. F. W. Murnau's* Nosferatu *(Prana 1922)*

Vlad belonged to the Order of the Dragon and from that came his name "Drakula", literally meaning of Drakul, the Dragon. Lee is sure that Stoker must have come across Vlad in his researches for *Dracula* and thus hit upon the name for the Vampire.

Vampire films made little headway at first. Although the Wizard of Montreuil, Georges Méliès, used camera trickery to turn himself first into a giant bat and then into Mephistopheles in *The Devil's Castle* in 1896, this was almost certainly not a Vampire film but merely Méliès indulging himself as actor, director and film visionary. In 1908, however, *Legend of a Ghost* was released. This movie, about a young girl's trip into Hell to get some magic water so as to bring a spectre back to life, tells of her battles in the Underworld with dragons and vampires and this probably makes *Legend of a Ghost* the first real film of the genre.

In 1914, Eclair Films produced *The Vampire* in which a psychologist is bound by a mysterious order's oath to kill his second wife by means of narcotics and "a huge vampire bat"! The Hungarian film *Drakula*, a silent version of Stoker's novel directed by Karoly Lathjay, has, unfortunately, vanished, and it was left to F. W. Murnau, with *Nosferatu: Eine Symphonie des Grauens*, to be the first major film-maker to bring Dracula to the screen, in 1922.

Murnau had already made a version of Robert Louis Stevenson's *Dr Jekyll and Mr Hyde* called *Der Januskopf* in 1920. But because he had neglected to clear copyright on the story, the film had to be destroyed. Undaunted, Murnau proceeded to make his version of *Dracula* and, although he carefully changed names and locations, Stoker's widow was able to bring a successful action against the director and all copies of the film were ordered to be destroyed. Fortunately for horror addicts, prints survive which show the Vampire, his name changed to Graf Orlok (played by Max Schreck) as

the most physically repulsive of all screen Vampires. His head is a skull, his eyes set deep in black sockets, his mouth an open black "O" in which are set teeth like a rat's and his long claw-like fingers are made more hideous by his fingernails which extend like talons. It is easy to believe that this Dracula is one of the Undead: it is harder to believe that he was ever one of the living even when he springs up from his rat-infested coffin on board ship to Bremen, which replaces the Whitby of Stoker's novel.

The plot is relatively unchanged, with Hutter (Stoker's Renfield) visiting the Count in his home in the Carpathian mountains. The scenes of horror are very effective, particularly the ship of the dead sailing into Bremen with the corpse of the Captain roped to the wheel, the scenes of the plague spread by Orlok through Bremen, and, earlier in the film, Orlok licking the blood from Hutter's cut thumb, a far more explicit scene of blood lust than Lugosi's gleaming eyes in *Dracula* as he sees the blood on Renfield's finger. Murnau's cameraman, Fritz Arno Wagner, makes good use of double exposure for the death of the Vampire as he is lured into the rays of the rising sun by Hutter's wife Ellen.

The film is in many ways untypical of Murnau and the German cinema style of the day, eschewing the use of expressionistic sets and camera angles in favour of real locations for the castle and for Bremen. This paid off in contrasting the evil appearance and actions of Graf Orlok with the sometimes prosaic backgrounds in which he moved.

In 1927, Tod Browning directed Lon Chaney Sr as a Vampire in *London After Midnight*, but for the first and by no means the last time he underestimated the mentality of his audience by inserting a "cheat ending" which showed the grotesque Vampire played by Chaney to be a creation of disguise and not the manifestation of the supernatural.

Chaney played a dual role in the film, that of the Vampire-like Phantom and also Chief Inspector Burke of Scotland Yard, thereby saving MGM the cost of an extra salary! The film itself is a fairly conventional murder mystery, well played by Conrad Nagel and Edna Tichenor as the Phantom's ghostly daughter Luna who prowls the moors around the Balfour estate with Chaney. Until the final unmasking of Chaney as an all-too-human actor, the macabre scenes are effective, and real Vampire lore is evident in the punctures above a victim's jugular vein and a corpse traditionally

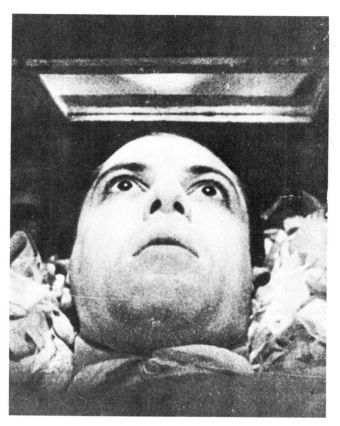

staked through the heart. If the film is a let-down, it is because of Browning's refusal to let the legend of the Vampire survive, as he was to do in 1930 when he made *Dracula*. Browning went on record to justify the ending when he averred: "*London After Midnight* is an example of how to get people to accept ghosts and other supernatural spirits by letting them turn out to be the machinations of a detective. Thereby the audience is not asked to believe the horrible impossible, but the horrible possible, and plausibility increases, rather than lessens, the thrills and chills."

In *London After Midnight*, the "Man of a Thousand Faces" suffered even more than usual to create a genuinely eerie and terrifying make-up: his Vampire was achieved by the use of specially made animal-like teeth which he could only stand to wear for short periods of time and which made it impossible for him to speak. He made his eyes bulge grotesquely by forcing them out of their sockets with thin wires: the effect as he prowled, with top hat and cape, was truly horrifying.

A bizarre film *Vampyr*, directed by Dane Carl Dreyer in France and privately financed by a young movie buff, Baron Nicholas de Gunzburg, turned out to be a minor horror masterpiece. Dreyer and scenarist Christen Jul freely adapted Sheridan Le Fanu's *Carmilla*, making the result a personal vision of the legend of the Vampire feeding after death on the living. Even the use of non-professional actors in the film—the film's producer Baron de Gunzburg played the hero David Gray under the stage name of Julian West—does not detract from its overall bleached-out horror and dream-like air of unreality.

Visually, the film matches its mood of suggested terror. It was shot by Rudolph Mate who achieved the eerie, dreamy quality of the movie by shooting scenes through a piece of gauze held some three feet in front of the lens. The uneasy quality that the images give was reinforced by Dreyer's deliberate paring down of the dialogue to a minimum. *Vampyr* is still a powerful film and very much unique in the annals of the horror genre.

As Dreyer was making *Vampyr* in France, Tod Browning was directing Lugosi in *Dracula* at Universal Studios. The first era of the Vampire film had ended. For the next 26 years, until Christopher Lee took up Count Dracula's cape in Terence Fisher's *Dracula* in 1957, Bela Lugosi would be evil personified and the cinema's Count Dracula.

DRACULA IS BORN: BELA

" I am Dracula . . . I bid you welcome!" When Bela Lugosi spoke these classic words, in the 1931 version of *Dracula*, he not only established himself as the screen's first Count Dracula but also, prophetically, spoke his own screen epitaph. After *Dracula*, Lugosi found himself firmly typecast: in the eyes of moviegoers everywhere, he was the archetypal Count Dracula, a star of horror films and, with few exceptions, his career as a straight actor was over.

Lugosi soon realized this. In April, 1933, barely two years after the release of *Dracula*, he said: "I can blame it all on Dracula. When I made my stage debut in New York, after leaving Hungary, I played a sympathetic role. Then came *Dracula* and I've been Dracula ever since. Since then Hollywood has scribbled a little card of classification for me and it looks as though I'll never be able to prove my mettle in any other kind of role."

When filming of *Dracula* was completed in October, 1930, Universal had no idea that the film would be the box-office success it turned out to be (it was the top grossing film of 1931). Nor did they realize that *Dracula* would be the forerunner of all the "classic" and successful horror movies to

LUGOSI

Far left. *Unmasked! Count Dracula (Bela Lugosi) and Vampire Hunter Van Helsing (Edward Van Sloan).* Dracula *(Universal 1931).* Below. Bela Lugosi *and Elizabeth Allen in* Mark of The Vampire *(MGM 1935)*

come in the 1940s. Indeed, with the completed picture on their hands, studio executives were apprehensive as to the effect the film's "horrific" content would have on its audiences, and, more importantly, on its takings. They finally compromised: the horror elements were played down and instead they emphasized the film's romantic and sexual aspects. So, in November, 1930, Universal took an advertisement in *The Motion Picture Herald* to promote *Dracula*: "The story of the strangest passion the world has ever known."

Becoming somewhat bolder, the Studio then told the Trade: "*Dracula* will get you if you don't watch out. The Universal thriller with the box-office grip. The crimson kiss of Dracula will thrill them to the core!" For the public, however, the first modern horror film was heralded rather more cautiously as: "The Strangest Love a Man Has Ever Known!"

By the time he made *Dracula*, Lugosi was no stranger to movies. He had already appeared in silent films in his native Hungary and in Germany, and had made a dozen or so pictures in New York and Hollywood.

By 1931, when *Oh, For a Man*, Lugosi's last pre-

Dracula film was released, he had already starred on Broadway in the stage version of *Dracula*. He had read for the part in July, 1927, and it had opened in September of the same year at the Fulton Theatre, New York. Lugosi's Dracula was born that night: he was to play the role on Broadway until the play closed there on May 19, 1928, after which he took the play on tour, playing Dracula in Los Angeles in June and returning again to California in 1929.

Horace Liveright had seen a London production of *Dracula* by Hamilton Deane in March, 1927, and commissioned John Balderston, then London correspondent on the New York *World* to adapt the play for America. (Balderston, incidentally, was later to work in Hollywood on *Frankenstein*, *Bride of Frankenstein* and *The Mummy*.) Edward Van Sloan played Van Helsing, as he would do in the film, Lugosi *was* Dracula and history was made.

As ever, the critics were less than enthusiastic, although Brooks Atkinson in the *New York Times* said: ". . . *Dracula* holds its audience nervously expectant . . . *Dracula* could doubtless scare the skeptics out of several years' growth into complete submission." Ronald Coleman in the *New York*

Mirror added: "Bela Lugosi is first rate as the vampire."

Universal Pictures had first considered the possibility of filming *Dracula* when it opened on the stage, but it was not until the coming of sound made the film technically easier, and censorship less likely to prove a problem, that the Studio finally decided to go ahead. They paid $40,000 for the rights to the story. Writers were engaged to ready *Dracula* for the screen and the search began for the actor to play the title role.

Although Lugosi had successfully created the part of the Count on Broadway, he was not Universal's first choice for the screen role. They felt, wrongly, that he was not sufficiently well known. Other names were put forward, but after Lugosi made a screen test for Universal he was signed. Filming began on September 29, 1930. Dwight Frye played Renfield, Edward Van Sloan repeated his role as Van Helsing, Helen Chandler played Mina Seward, David Manners, Jonathan Harker. The superb gothic sets were designed by Charles D. Hall, the scenario was credited to Garrett Fort and Tod Browning, directed with more flair and nerve than he had shown in *London After Midnight*. This time there were to be no more "cheat endings".

The film begins with a scene that was to become "traditional" in the horror genre—a lonely coach ride through lowering forests and stark cliffs and rocks. Renfield in the coach only stops briefly at an inn where he is given a crucifix to wear for "his mother's sake" before he continues his journey to Castle Dracula. From then on the horror builds up. Scene after scene stays in the memory and still retains its power to chill. In particular, the menace is felt in the first appearance of the Count, with the camera dissolving through a view of the castle into crypts full of cobwebs until it tracks through the arches to stop in front of a coffin. Slowly the coffin lid moves and begins to open, and Dracula's hand starts to emerge.

After meeting Dracula, his three dead wives, white-faced and evil, are seen among the cobwebs and the cold, dark stones. But the real horror of the castle held together by death and spider webs is not realized until Renfield arrives, after a terror-filled drive in Dracula's coach, with no driver except a bat hovering over the galloping horses. Here Lugosi's presence, Browning's direction and the eerie and magnificent photography of Karl Freund combine to produce a succession of scenes which are the best in the film. Down a huge stair-case, on which beetles and armadillos scuttle, Dracula, polite menace in his immaculate evening dress, opera cloak and an accent which has become standard Transylvanian over the years, comes slowly towards Renfield and announces: "I am Dracula."

There follows the howling of the wolves and Dracula's delighted comment: "Listen to them, the Children of the Night. What music they make!" In such an atmosphere it is hardly surprising that within a short while Renfield, infected with the bite of the Vampire, starts eating flies and spiders and pleads with Dracula to be allowed to progress to more substantial meals.

It is Renfield who supervises Count Dracula's sea voyage from Transylvania to England and it is here, when the film leaves the haunted vaults of Castle Dracula, that it loses much of its atmosphere and chill. The voyage of the Vesta is muffed by Browning who used stock shots of the film *Head Winds* with a superimposed title "Aboard the Vesta—Bound for England". He ignored the horror implicit in a situation where, during the voyage, Dracula kills all the crew, one by one, so that the Vesta reaches Grimsby with a dead crew and the Captain strapped lifeless at the wheel. Instead, Browning cuts after Dracula goes up on deck to some days later when the ship of the dead drifts into Grimsby. It is left to Browning as Narrator to explain that the crew has vanished and the Captain has been found dead at the wheel.

The loss in horror momentum continues when Dracula rents Carfax Abbey, although there is much pleasure to be gained by his disinterest in repairing the ruins of his new home. "It reminds me of the broken battlements of my own castle in Transylvania!" There is a genuine dislocation in mood when Dracula is in London: from the mediaeval mise-en-scène of the Transylvanian portion, it is a shock, and does the film no good, to find Dracula and ourselves among cars and modern clothes and almost contemporary (1930) theatre-goers.

There are two things about the film which seem strange against the more modern Vampire films. The Count has no fangs, and no blood—apart from the scene when Renfield pricks his finger in Castle Dracula—is ever seen. When Dracula metamorphoses from bat into Count in Lucy's bedroom, the scene is faded away as Lugosi stoops to bite the sleeping girl's neck.

15

Above. *Bela Lugosi and Carol Borland survey a body in Tod Browning's* Mark of The Vampire *(MGM 1935)*
Right. *Miss Borland strikes a pose as Luna, the 'Vampire Girl' in the same movie*

Other isolated scenes stand out: Van Helsing looking into a polished cigarette box and seeing that Dracula casts no reflection; Lucy in white gown and shrouded with mist being enveloped by Dracula's cloak in a movement both horrifying and sexual in its impact; the battle of wills between Dracula and Van Helsing culminating in Van Helsing resisting the commands of the Vampire to approach and instead, in a scene of release, defeating Dracula's attack with the power of the crucifix. But the film ends on an anticlimax as Browning, once more losing his nerve at a crucial scene, leaves Van Helsing to despatch Dracula with the customary stake through his heart—off screen, so that Dracula's death consists of Lugosi uttering a none-too-convincing groan on the soundtrack. Some amends are made by Van Helsing's final address to the audience, apparently on a proscenium stage with a cinema screen behind him. In an absolutely serious tone of voice, he says:

"Please! One moment! Just a word before you go. We hope the memories of *Dracula* won't give you bad dreams—so just a word of reassurance! When you get home tonight and lights have been turned out and you're afraid to look behind the curtains—and you dread to see a face appear at the window—why, just pull yourselves together and remember . . . that, after all, there are such things!"

Although the film no longer stands up in its entirety to re-viewing now, there are parts of it which have never been bettered in Vampire films,

and in Lugosi's performance there is something which transcends the passage of time. From his first appearance on the enormous stairs as he breaks through a giant cobweb to greet the unwary Renfield and, particularly, in the Transylvanian scenes, he makes his Count Dracula the definitive performance—until Christopher Lee's portrayal over a quarter of a century later. Lugosi has a great deal going for him, and where director and script allow, he takes full advantage. His accent—thick and syrupy and still "standard Transylvanian" for impressionists—is absolutely right. The evening dress and cloak in which he moves around the cavernous rooms and corridors of Castle Dracula make for an added frisson of unease, and he is able to use his height—he was 6 ft. 1 in.—effectively in his scenes, particularly in his "duels" with Edward Van Sloan as Van Helsing.

The film is not successful as horror throughout its length. Much is the fault of the script, which inevitably owed more to the play than to Stoker's original novel, and of Tod Browning's inexplicable tendency to cut away at climactic moments. Much of the most terrifying footage, in particular the camera prowling through webbed crypts and massive walls, shows the imprint of cameraman Karl Freund who brought to the film much of the poetic feel and visual style of the Impressionist German cinema in which he had trained. There is little doubt that the first portion of the film is the most horrific—after the voyage to Grimsby, the saving grace is Lugosi's performance which has

to battle through very static staging and long expositionary dialogue scenes. He is abetted ably by Dwight Frye as Renfield, growing progressively more crazy, scuttling like a demonic rat towards the Seward's maid as if to bite her neck or supervising the transport of Dracula's coffins from Transylvania to England. Edward Van Sloan makes a suitably powerful antagonist as Van Helsing, armed with crucifix and wolfbane and uttering one of the classic lines from horror movies: "I may be able to bring you proof that the superstition of yesterday can become the scientific reality of today!"

Dracula was Lugosi's film and with it, he became a star.

The critics, as ever, had considerable reservations about the film; and, as ever, the film withstood all their assaults, going on to make a fortune for Universal Pictures, if not for Lugosi who received a mere $3500—$500 a week for the seven weeks the film took to shoot. The *New York Herald Tribune* wrote on February 13, 1931, that Lugosi was, "even more effective than he was on the stage, which is something of a tribute", a sentiment echoed by the *Hollywood Filmograph* on April 4, 1931: "Lugosi outdoes any of the performances of the undead count which we have seen him give on the stage. There are times when the force of the evil vampire seems to sweep from him beyond the confines of the screen and into the minds of the audience. His cruel smile—hypnotic glance—slow, stately tread, they make *Dracula*."

Although Lugosi went on to make other horror movies, all showing a decline in quality and horror, he did not essay the role of a Vampire again until four years later when he was directed again by Tod Browning in MGM's re-make of *London After Midnight*, called *The Mark of the Vampire*. The film's basic plot was a straight "pinch" from *Dracula* although the screenwriters Guy Endore and Bernard Schubert made some necessary changes: the locale was moved from Transylvania to Czechoslovakia, Count Dracula was changed to

Above left. Lugosi makes his final bow at Universal Studios for Abbott and Costello Meet Frankenstein *(Universal 1948)*
Top. The vengeful Dr. Carruthers (Bela Lugosi) animates his killer Vampire in The Devil Bat *(PRC 1940)*

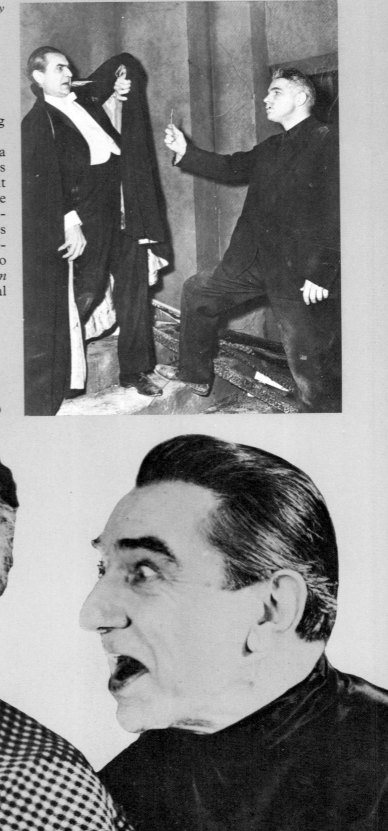

Right. *Cross purposes. Bela Lugosi as Armand Tesla backs away from Matt Willis' crucifix in* Return of The Vampire *(Columbia 1943)*
Below. *The Attack of The British 'B' Movie! Lugosi with Arthur Lucan in* Mother Riley Meets The Vampire *(Renown 1952)*

Count Mora and Lionel Barrymore's Van Helsing character became Professor Zelen.

The film was not good, either as horror or as a Vampire movie. Once more Tod Browning's direction and the script were weak links and what effect the film does have comes from the good use of a comparatively lavish MGM budget, the excellent art direction of Cedric Gibbons, and James Wong Howe's moody and atmospheric cinematography. Browning once more went back to the basic mistake he had made in 1927 with *London After Midnight*—he jettisoned the supernatural genesis of the Vampire in favour of an ending that once more showed all the so-called Vampire happenings as no more than the prosaic deeds of a troupe of vaudeville performers hired by the villain. The deliberate and counterproductive "cheat ending" satisfied neither those who wanted the supernatural they had got from *Dracula* nor those who wanted to see a straight thriller. Lugosi was used as "himself", a Vampire "prop", with no chance to use his distinctive voice until the last scenes in the film when, speaking to the "Vampire Girl" (Carol Borland) he says: "This vampire business has given me a great idea for a new act, Luna. In this new act, I will be the Vampire. Did you watch me? I gave all of me—I was greater than any real vampire!" He was not, however, and the film is a loss, made only bearable by Carol Borland as Luna, sweeping over the set in her bat-wings, occasional filmic episodes such as Carol Borland snarling at ingenue Elizabeth Allen, and

some splendidly lit and photographed sets and fog-laden scenes.

His next Vampire movie, made five years later in 1940, saw Lugosi even further in decline as a Vampire star. This time he did not even have the salvation of MGM production values to help him through *The Devil Bat*. The film was one of the many Lugosi made for "Poverty Row" film producers, in this case the home of the bad B-feature, PRC (Producers Releasing Corporation). Directed by Jean Yarbrough, Lugosi played crazed Dr. Paul Caruthers, who, bent on demonic revenge against his employers, creates giant Vampire bats trained to attack at the scent of a shaving lotion devised by Lugosi. The best thing in an otherwise dire movie is the growth of the Devil Bat, created in best mad-scientist tradition by strange "electric radiation". The soundtrack shrieks which accompany the bat on its killer flights through the night, and Lugosi's injunction to his

Fangs ain't what they used to be! In the same movie, Lugosi takes the tube while Ian Wilson looks on

Aged 62, Lugosi reflects on his British stage tour of Dracula *in this publicity still*

future victims as he gives them the shaving lotion to put it "on the tender part of your neck" and his very ripe "Good-bye" which follows, are indeed memorable. However, Lugosi must have been relieved when, naturally, he fell victim to one of his own creations.

He was back as a thinly disguised Count Dracula, in this case for copyright reasons called Armand Tesla, in Columbia's *The Return of The Vampire*. Directed by Lew Landers, it was little improvement on *The Devil Bat* although Lugosi's role was much nearer to the one he had made his own in *Dracula*.

Lugosi is killed twice in the movie, the first time in 1918 when Lady Jane Ainsley (Frieda Inescort) impales him with an iron stake. Never a studio to miss contemporary relevance, Columbia had the Vampire's grave disturbed by a Nazi bomb (the film was made in 1944) and workmen, believing that the stake through the corpse was a result of the bombing, remove it. The Vampire is off on its rampage again. Once more he enslaves his hairy-faced helper, Andreas (Matt Willis), luring him from his clean-shaven post as a laboratory assistant. It is his mistake, since, after his revengeful attacks upon those who had caused his first death, Andreas forces Tesla into the sunlight where he disintegrates. This scene is easily the best in the film and achieves real horror as the flesh melts and runs to show the grinning skull beneath. This was achieved by moulding a wax face over a skull and allowing it to melt, and the British Censor, ever mindful of his place as the devisor of the "H" (for horrific) certificate, insisted that the Vampire should perish with the less horrifying stake through the heart. The special effects which turned Matt Willis into the werewolf were well done too, but the film merely emphasized Lugosi's inexorable decline as a screen Vampire.

Lugosi was really unlucky. Where other "classic" monsters were finally despatched (as far as Universal Pictures were concerned) by meeting Abbott and Costello, Lugosi not only met this dreadful pair of monster killers in 1948 in *Abbott and Costello Meet Frankenstein* but received an even worse fate later at the hands of English comic Arthur Lucan in *Mother Riley Meets the Vampire*. These two dismal films were Bela Lugosi's last appearances as a Vampire and they are unworthy memorials to the screen's first Count Dracula.

Abbott and Costello Meet Frankenstein was the last time Lugosi was to work at Universal Studios.

Shooting began on St. Valentine's Day, 1948, 17 years after the opening of *Dracula* in New York. Despite that omen, the film never took off.

The plot of the movie was as simple as its two titular stars. Count Dracula, now the owner of the Frankenstein Creature (Glenn Strange), decides to replace the Creature's damaged brain with the brain of an idiot which he can then dominate. Not surprisingly, he picks upon Lou Costello as a suitable donor. However, the Fates are on the side of Abbott and Costello as the Wolfman (Lon Chaney Jr.) is once more in pursuit of Count Dracula, finally pursuing him and, catching him just as he turns into a bat, the two of them plunge over a parapet to their deaths.

The film failed to do what Lugosi had hoped for: pave the way for a sequel to *Dracula*. In 1952, he found himself in England, making his last and most awful appearance as a Vampire in *Mother Riley Meets The Vampire*. Released in America as *Vampire Over London* in 1953 and again in 1964 as *My Son, The Vampire*, it had Lugosi as Von Housen, the Vampire in search of a large deposit of uranium and using a metal robot to aid him in his schemes. The robot falls into the hands of Old Mother Riley (in reality, a female impersonator, Arthur Lucan) and the film, in which, despite its title, Lugosi only believes himself to be a Vampire, is a poor British screen farce.

Lugosi's last years were as horrific as any of his screen parts. In 1955 he was committed to the Metropolitan State Hospital at Norwalk, California to try to shake his addiction to narcotics. Here Hope Liniger, a studio editing department clerk, used to write to her idol, signing her letters "Dash of Hope". Lugosi was released on August 2, 1955, after 105 days in hospital. On August 25, he was married to Hope. It was Lugosi's fifth and final marriage.

Hope Lugosi found her husband dead on August 16, 1956; he was 74 and, in one last macabre touch to a life and career marked by strangeness, Lugosi was buried in his Dracula cape, according to his own wishes.

But if his life was marred, *Dracula* remains as a great memorial to the screen's first Count Dracula. For all of us who are afficionados of horror and Vampire films, Lugosi remains pristine, slick black hair, immaculate evening dress and cape, gliding among the spider webs and ruined battlements of Castle Dracula, the eternal Vampire with the true voice of horror.

Between 1952 and 1958 only minor horror movies appeared and by 1958, the Vampire film seemed totally in decline. But Dracula, more impressively than ever before, was to return from Britain, in the form of the tall, gaunt and handsome Christopher Lee.

1956 had seen Hammer's colour production *The Curse of Frankenstein*. Directed by Terence Fisher, what had started as a "sleeper" had turned out to be a runaway success. Even more auspiciously, *The Curse of Frankenstein* made two new international horror stars—Peter Cushing, who played Baron Frankenstein, and Christopher Lee, who, following Boris Karloff's example, played the Creature. It was only natural, then, after that success, that Sir James Carreras, Chairman of Hammer films, should choose to re-make *Dracula* as his next horror project.

Christopher Lee was the natural choice for the part of Count Dracula. He was able to bring to the role the looks and height and immense personal charm that was to make his Count Dracula definitive for people who had never seen a horror movie or for whom Bela Lugosi was a flickering shadow briefly glimpsed on late night movies. Lee was also able to add something more to his portrayal, his superb voice that forever eradicated the Middle-European cadences for a new cinema generation that up to then had been the standard Transylvanian accent.

The behind-the-camera team responsible for the breakthrough of *The Curse of Frankenstein*—cameraman Jack Asher, composer James Bernard, screen-writer Jimmy Sangster and director Terence Fisher—were joined on *Dracula* by the brilliant art director Bernard Robinson. Sangster adapted the Stoker novel to great effect, excising the diversions that slowed the 1931 film and producing a taut, compelling narrative. The covert symbolism of the Lugosi film was replaced with terror and

Below. *Christopher Lee as The Count perishes in the water in* Dracula, Prince of Darkness *(Hammer-Seven Arts 1965)*
Opposite. *Christopher Lee as Frankenstein's Monster, Hammer-style in* The Curse of Frankenstein *(Hammer 1956)*

future victims as he gives them the shaving lotion to put it "on the tender part of your neck" and his very ripe "Good-bye" which follows, are indeed memorable. However, Lugosi must have been relieved when, naturally, he fell victim to one of his own creations.

He was back as a thinly disguised Count Dracula, in this case for copyright reasons called Armand Tesla, in Columbia's *The Return of The Vampire*. Directed by Lew Landers, it was little improvement on *The Devil Bat* although Lugosi's role was much nearer to the one he had made his own in *Dracula*.

Lugosi is killed twice in the movie, the first time in 1918 when Lady Jane Ainsley (Frieda Inescort) impales him with an iron stake. Never a studio to miss contemporary relevance, Columbia had the Vampire's grave disturbed by a Nazi bomb (the film was made in 1944) and workmen, believing that the stake through the corpse was a result of the bombing, remove it. The Vampire is off on its rampage again. Once more he enslaves his hairy-faced helper, Andreas (Matt Willis), luring him from his clean-shaven post as a laboratory assistant. It is his mistake, since, after his revengeful attacks upon those who had caused his first death, Andreas forces Tesla into the sunlight where he disintegrates. This scene is easily the best in the film and achieves real horror as the flesh melts and runs to show the grinning skull beneath. This was achieved by moulding a wax face over a skull and allowing it to melt, and the British Censor, ever mindful of his place as the devisor of the "H" (for horrific) certificate, insisted that the Vampire should perish with the less horrifying stake through the heart. The special effects which turned Matt Willis into the werewolf were well done too, but the film merely emphasized Lugosi's inexorable decline as a screen Vampire.

Lugosi was really unlucky. Where other "classic" monsters were finally despatched (as far as Universal Pictures were concerned) by meeting Abbott and Costello, Lugosi not only met this dreadful pair of monster killers in 1948 in *Abbott and Costello Meet Frankenstein* but received an even worse fate later at the hands of English comic Arthur Lucan in *Mother Riley Meets the Vampire*. These two dismal films were Bela Lugosi's last appearances as a Vampire and they are unworthy memorials to the screen's first Count Dracula.

Abbott and Costello Meet Frankenstein was the last time Lugosi was to work at Universal Studios.

Shooting began on St. Valentine's Day, 1948, 17 years after the opening of *Dracula* in New York. Despite that omen, the film never took off.

The plot of the movie was as simple as its two titular stars. Count Dracula, now the owner of the Frankenstein Creature (Glenn Strange), decides to replace the Creature's damaged brain with the brain of an idiot which he can then dominate. Not surprisingly, he picks upon Lou Costello as a suitable donor. However, the Fates are on the side of Abbott and Costello as the Wolfman (Lon Chaney Jr.) is once more in pursuit of Count Dracula, finally pursuing him and, catching him just as he turns into a bat, the two of them plunge over a parapet to their deaths.

The film failed to do what Lugosi had hoped for: pave the way for a sequel to *Dracula*. In 1952, he found himself in England, making his last and most awful appearance as a Vampire in *Mother Riley Meets The Vampire*. Released in America as *Vampire Over London* in 1953 and again in 1964 as *My Son, The Vampire*, it had Lugosi as Von Housen, the Vampire in search of a large deposit of uranium and using a metal robot to aid him in his schemes. The robot falls into the hands of Old Mother Riley (in reality, a female impersonator, Arthur Lucan) and the film, in which, despite its title, Lugosi only believes himself to be a Vampire, is a poor British screen farce.

Lugosi's last years were as horrific as any of his screen parts. In 1955 he was committed to the Metropolitan State Hospital at Norwalk, California to try to shake his addiction to narcotics. Here Hope Liniger, a studio editing department clerk, used to write to her idol, signing her letters "Dash of Hope". Lugosi was released on August 2, 1955, after 105 days in hospital. On August 25, he was married to Hope. It was Lugosi's fifth and final marriage.

Hope Lugosi found her husband dead on August 16, 1956; he was 74 and, in one last macabre touch to a life and career marked by strangeness, Lugosi was buried in his Dracula cape, according to his own wishes.

But if his life was marred, *Dracula* remains as a great memorial to the screen's first Count Dracula. For all of us who are afficionados of horror and Vampire films, Lugosi remains pristine, slick black hair, immaculate evening dress and cape, gliding among the spider webs and ruined battlements of Castle Dracula, the eternal Vampire with the true voice of horror.

Between 1952 and 1958 only minor horror movies appeared and by 1958, the Vampire film seemed totally in decline. But Dracula, more impressively than ever before, was to return from Britain, in the form of the tall, gaunt and handsome Christopher Lee.

1956 had seen Hammer's colour production *The Curse of Frankenstein*. Directed by Terence Fisher, what had started as a "sleeper" had turned out to be a runaway success. Even more auspiciously, *The Curse of Frankenstein* made two new international horror stars—Peter Cushing, who played Baron Frankenstein, and Christopher Lee, who, following Boris Karloff's example, played the Creature. It was only natural, then, after that success, that Sir James Carreras, Chairman of Hammer films, should choose to re-make *Dracula* as his next horror project.

Christopher Lee was the natural choice for the part of Count Dracula. He was able to bring to the role the looks and height and immense personal charm that was to make his Count Dracula definitive for people who had never seen a horror movie or for whom Bela Lugosi was a flickering shadow briefly glimpsed on late night movies. Lee was also able to add something more to his portrayal, his superb voice that forever eradicated the Middle-European cadences for a new cinema generation that up to then had been the standard Transylvanian accent.

The behind-the-camera team responsible for the breakthrough of *The Curse of Frankenstein*—cameraman Jack Asher, composer James Bernard, screen-writer Jimmy Sangster and director Terence Fisher—were joined on *Dracula* by the brilliant art director Bernard Robinson. Sangster adapted the Stoker novel to great effect, excising the diversions that slowed the 1931 film and producing a taut, compelling narrative. The covert symbolism of the Lugosi film was replaced with terror and

Below. *Christopher Lee as The Count perishes in the water in* Dracula, Prince of Darkness *(Hammer-Seven Arts 1965)*
Opposite. *Christopher Lee as Frankenstein's Monster, Hammer-style in* The Curse of Frankenstein *(Hammer 1956)*

future victims as he gives them the shaving lotion to put it "on the tender part of your neck" and his very ripe "Good-bye" which follows, are indeed memorable. However, Lugosi must have been relieved when, naturally, he fell victim to one of his own creations.

He was back as a thinly disguised Count Dracula, in this case for copyright reasons called Armand Tesla, in Columbia's *The Return of The Vampire*. Directed by Lew Landers, it was little improvement on *The Devil Bat* although Lugosi's role was much nearer to the one he had made his own in *Dracula*.

Lugosi is killed twice in the movie, the first time in 1918 when Lady Jane Ainsley (Frieda Inescort) impales him with an iron stake. Never a studio to miss contemporary relevance, Columbia had the Vampire's grave disturbed by a Nazi bomb (the film was made in 1944) and workmen, believing that the stake through the corpse was a result of the bombing, remove it. The Vampire is off on its rampage again. Once more he enslaves his hairy-faced helper, Andreas (Matt Willis), luring him from his clean-shaven post as a laboratory assistant. It is his mistake, since, after his revengeful attacks upon those who had caused his first death, Andreas forces Tesla into the sunlight where he disintegrates. This scene is easily the best in the film and achieves real horror as the flesh melts and runs to show the grinning skull beneath. This was achieved by moulding a wax face over a skull and allowing it to melt, and the British Censor, ever mindful of his place as the devisor of the "H" (for horrific) certificate, insisted that the Vampire should perish with the less horrifying stake through the heart. The special effects which turned Matt Willis into the werewolf were well done too, but the film merely emphasized Lugosi's inexorable decline as a screen Vampire.

Lugosi was really unlucky. Where other "classic" monsters were finally despatched (as far as Universal Pictures were concerned) by meeting Abbott and Costello, Lugosi not only met this dreadful pair of monster killers in 1948 in *Abbott and Costello Meet Frankenstein* but received an even worse fate later at the hands of English comic Arthur Lucan in *Mother Riley Meets the Vampire*. These two dismal films were Bela Lugosi's last appearances as a Vampire and they are unworthy memorials to the screen's first Count Dracula.

Abbott and Costello Meet Frankenstein was the last time Lugosi was to work at Universal Studios.

Shooting began on St. Valentine's Day, 1948, 17 years after the opening of *Dracula* in New York. Despite that omen, the film never took off.

The plot of the movie was as simple as its two titular stars. Count Dracula, now the owner of the Frankenstein Creature (Glenn Strange), decides to replace the Creature's damaged brain with the brain of an idiot which he can then dominate. Not surprisingly, he picks upon Lou Costello as a suitable donor. However, the Fates are on the side of Abbott and Costello as the Wolfman (Lon Chaney Jr.) is once more in pursuit of Count Dracula, finally pursuing him and, catching him just as he turns into a bat, the two of them plunge over a parapet to their deaths.

The film failed to do what Lugosi had hoped for: pave the way for a sequel to *Dracula*. In 1952, he found himself in England, making his last and most awful appearance as a Vampire in *Mother Riley Meets The Vampire*. Released in America as *Vampire Over London* in 1953 and again in 1964 as *My Son, The Vampire*, it had Lugosi as Von Housen, the Vampire in search of a large deposit of uranium and using a metal robot to aid him in his schemes. The robot falls into the hands of Old Mother Riley (in reality, a female impersonator, Arthur Lucan) and the film, in which, despite its title, Lugosi only believes himself to be a Vampire, is a poor British screen farce.

Lugosi's last years were as horrific as any of his screen parts. In 1955 he was committed to the Metropolitan State Hospital at Norwalk, California to try to shake his addiction to narcotics. Here Hope Liniger, a studio editing department clerk, used to write to her idol, signing her letters "Dash of Hope". Lugosi was released on August 2, 1955, after 105 days in hospital. On August 25, he was married to Hope. It was Lugosi's fifth and final marriage.

Hope Lugosi found her husband dead on August 16, 1956; he was 74 and, in one last macabre touch to a life and career marked by strangeness, Lugosi was buried in his Dracula cape, according to his own wishes.

But if his life was marred, *Dracula* remains as a great memorial to the screen's first Count Dracula. For all of us who are afficionados of horror and Vampire films, Lugosi remains pristine, slick black hair, immaculate evening dress and cape, gliding among the spider webs and ruined battlements of Castle Dracula, the eternal Vampire with the true voice of horror.

etween 1952 and 1958 only minor horror movies appeared and by 1958, the Vampire film seemed totally in decline. But Dracula, more impressively than ever before, was to return from Britain, in the form of the tall, gaunt and handsome Christopher Lee.

1956 had seen Hammer's colour production *The Curse of Frankenstein*. Directed by Terence Fisher, what had started as a "sleeper" had turned out to be a runaway success. Even more auspiciously, *The Curse of Frankenstein* made two new international horror stars—Peter Cushing, who played Baron Frankenstein, and Christopher Lee, who, following Boris Karloff's example, played the Creature. It was only natural, then, after that success, that Sir James Carreras, Chairman of Hammer films, should choose to re-make *Dracula* as his next horror project.

Christopher Lee was the natural choice for the part of Count Dracula. He was able to bring to the role the looks and height and immense personal charm that was to make his Count Dracula definitive for people who had never seen a horror movie or for whom Bela Lugosi was a flickering shadow briefly glimpsed on late night movies. Lee was also able to add something more to his portrayal, his superb voice that forever eradicated the Middle-European cadences for a new cinema generation that up to then had been the standard Transylvanian accent.

The behind-the-camera team responsible for the breakthrough of *The Curse of Frankenstein*—cameraman Jack Asher, composer James Bernard, screen-writer Jimmy Sangster and director Terence Fisher—were joined on *Dracula* by the brilliant art director Bernard Robinson. Sangster adapted the Stoker novel to great effect, excising the diversions that slowed the 1931 film and producing a taut, compelling narrative. The covert symbolism of the Lugosi film was replaced with terror and

Below. *Christopher Lee as The Count perishes in the water in* Dracula, Prince of Darkness *(Hammer-Seven Arts 1965)*
Opposite. *Christopher Lee as Frankenstein's Monster, Hammer-style in* The Curse of Frankenstein *(Hammer 1956)*

Inset left. *John Carson, seen here with Peter Sallis, prepares to impale the sleeping Vampire (Isla Blair) in* Taste The Blood of Dracula *(Hammer 1970)*
Inset right. *The screen's most potent Van Helsing, Peter Cushing, confronts Christopher Lee with his human sacrifice Joanna Lumley in* The Satanic Rites of Dracula *(Hammer 1973)*
Below. *The Death of the Vampire as Lee ignites at the climax of Roy Ward Baker's* Scars of Dracula *(Hammer/EMI 1970)*

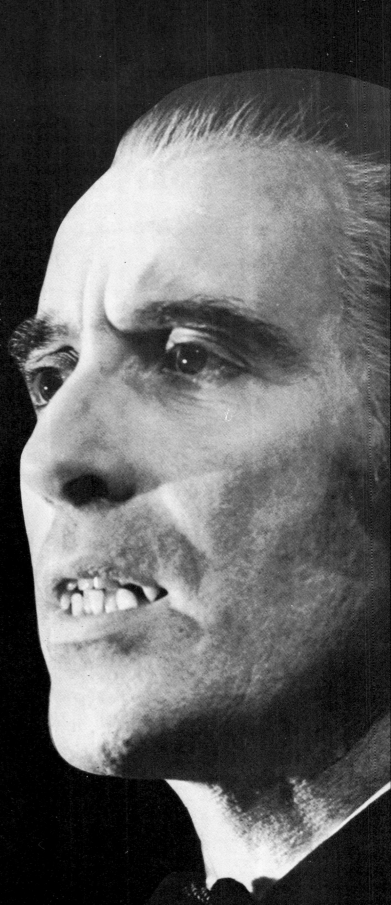

with a Dracula who had both innate evil and great personal attraction. Peter Cushing as a steely Van Helsing spoke the death-knell of the over-super-natural Dracula of Lugosi and Browning when he said: "It is a common fallacy that vampires can change into bats and wolves." Lee's Dracula was infinitely more terrible, not just for his blazing red eyes and ripping fangs but also because he was not just a monster—his was a portrayal of a man, a terrible and different man.

Fisher, who had deliberately not re-looked at Universal's *Dracula* before he made his own film, had no doubt as to how the Count should appear: "Dracula is tremendously sensual. This is one of the great physical as well as mental attractions of the Vampire. This is one of the great attractions of evil." Lee added to the part by putting in his own interpretation of the Count: "My own ideas were mainly concerned with the nobility of the man, his austerity. As well as being literally a demon, he must also be acceptable, a man of great philosophy and a man of great stillness. He must be, obviously, completely irresistible to women and as far as men are concerned, unstoppable, and that's what I tried to put into the character."

That Lee succeeded superbly is borne out by the film itself, 82 minutes of screen terror. Scene after scene stays in the memory: Harker (John Van Eyssen) entering the tomb of the sleeping vampire woman and driving a stake into the beautiful creature's heart; as the stake enters, a well of blood gushes into the camera and, terrifyingly, she is turned into a hideous old crone as death finally comes. Harker looks up, in triumph, only to find that the sun has now gone down, leaving him trapped with Dracula. The final battle between Van Helsing and Dracula was inspired by Peter Cushing who had suggested ". . . some sort of almost Douglas Fairbanks scene" as the two fought to the death. Because the set had already been built, Cushing ran along a long refectory table and leaped as far as he could, pulling the curtains from the windows to provide the sunlight which would kill Count Dracula. In an ending of sheer cinema magic, Cushing, using a crucifix created out of two crossed candlesticks, forces Lee into the pool of sunlight. The Count disintegrates horribly, until all that is left are some strands of hair, some dust, and the crimson signet ring of Dracula reflecting the sunlight.

Fisher's description of Lee's first appearance goes a long way to explain the actor's total dominance

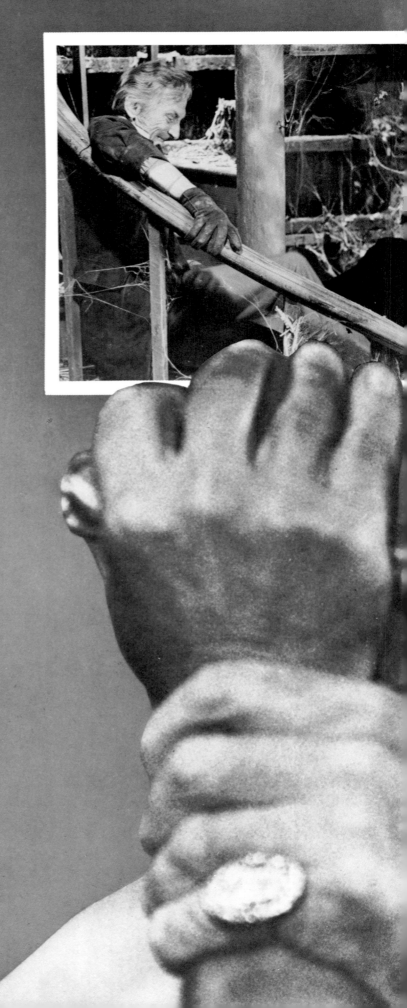

of the role in *Dracula* and his subsequent movies. Says Fisher: "The first time Dracula is seen, at the top of the staircase, in silhouette, the audience, the ones you want to laugh, start to laugh, because they think that they're going to see the fangs and everything else. Dracula comes downstairs, into close-up and they see this handsome, charming and totally attractive man." This was exactly as Lee appeared in *Dracula* and his performance, and that of Cushing as a more than worthy opponent, with Fisher's superb direction, made the film the finest Vampire movie ever made and totally successful.

It was not until 1965 that Lee appeared as Dracula again for Hammer—under the skilled direction of Terence Fisher—in *Dracula—Prince of Darkness*.

Once again Castle Dracula—or, to be more accurate, the first 20 feet of its gothic architecture, the rest of it being a triumph of glass shot special effects—rose again at the small British Bray Studios, home of the "classic" Hammer movies.

The film was good but by no means as good as *Dracula* had been. For one thing, Lee's Dracula no longer had an opponent of the acting calibre of Peter Cushing to play Van Helsing and without the interplay of characters that the two had provided in the former film, *Dracula—Prince of Darkness* lacked something. Director Fisher tried to make amends in what turned out to be the best part of the film—the re-use of the climactic duel and destruction of Dracula from *Dracula*, shown in a suitably cloud-wreathed frame, as a prologue to the movie.

After this opening, the story never really demanded a great deal from Lee, who did, however, take all the opportunities afforded him. Once more, Bernard Robinson provided an immaculate Carpathia through which Fisher drove his four visitors on the traditional Transylvanian coach ride. Abandoned at the crossroads by a superstitious driver who refused to take them nearer than two miles to Castle Dracula, they were conveyed there by a conveniently arriving, but driverless coach.

From then on, the film takes the standard Hammer paths: Philip Latham, as sinister man-servant Klove, slits open the stomach of Alan (Charles Tingwell) to reconstitute with blood the ashes of Count Dracula in a piece of special effects that is one of the film's high spots. The first to suffer willingly the Vampire's bite is Barbara Shelley, a much-used Hammer beauty, who then proceeds herself to make a rather charming Vampire. She dies when Father Sandor (Andrew

Keir) kills her, but not before she has bitten her fellow traveller Diana (Suzan Farmer).

Finally, Dracula perishes, this time by water as the ice floe on which he stands is systematically shot away by Father Sandor and he slips into the cold and deadly embrace of the moat that surrounds his own castle.

Freddie Francis, one-time cinematographer and Academy Award winner for his photography in *Sons and Lovers*, took over the directorial reins when Lee next donned his fangs and cloak in 1968 for *Dracula Has Risen From The Grave*. Francis' visual flair contributed some effective location sequences, in particular Christopher Lee and Veronica Carlson with their funeral coach in the lush greens of the Transylvania Forests (in reality, Black Park). The sexuality between the Count and his victims, Veronica Carlson and Barbara Ewing, is entirely overt and, in the little he has to do, Lee is superbly commanding and both totally magnetic and totally chilling in his evil. It is sad that he is not given enough to do in the film and once more lacks

the nemesis of Cushing's Van Helsing. Instead, revived from his living death under ice by the blood that trickles through the ice from a wound on a stunned priest's head, he is finally despatched this time after a struggle with the film's hero, Paul (Barry Andrews), when he is hurled over a mountain side to be impaled upon a gigantic cross.

Peter Sasdy, a horror movie director who never fulfilled early signs of promise, took Lee through his next screen incarnation as the Count in the first of two movies made by Lee in 1970, *Taste The Blood of Dracula*. The film was set, with no advantage, in Victorian England instead of Transylvania, where three brothel-frequenting gentlemen of depraved tastes and a craving for escape from their ennui, join Lord Courtley (Ralph Bates) to enable him to buy a cloak, a phial of dried blood and a signet ring, the remains of Dracula. Courtley perishes as he drinks the blood of Dracula, reconstituted from the contents of the phial, and Lee's gaunt and handsome Count Dracula is loose again. Dracula wreaks havoc, vampirizing two women,

Left. *Christopher Lee portrays the elderly Vampire Count as envisaged in Bram Stoker's original novel in the Jess Franco movie* Count Dracula *(Fenix/Corona/Filmar/Towers 1970)*
Below. *Corruption of the Vampire. Lee decays in Roy Ward Baker's* Scars of Dracula *(Hammer/EMI 1970)*

one of whom, in turn, bites her sweetheart, turning him into one of the Undead, until he is cornered in a chapel by the hero, there to be killed once more.

Sasdy gave Lee little to do in this movie, and in Roy Ward Baker's *The Scars of Dracula*, also made in 1970, there was still less for Lee, the actor, to get his teeth into. Director Baker showed little feel for either the gothic tradition of the Vampire movie or for the horror film, and so *The Scars of Dracula* suffered accordingly. The best moments are provided by Lee's icily formal Dracula, suddenly and alarmingly scaling the castle walls like a giant lizard pinned to the stones. Jenny Hanley provides an adequate heroine as Sarah Framsen, but once again Cushing as Van Helsing is sorely missed. The film, as usual, ends on one of its high points: this time the evil Count is killed by a real *deus ex machina* as a bolt of lightning strikes him as he is about to impale Denis Waterman, and he plunges, a living comet, on fire from the turrets.

Dracula A.D. 1972 released, appropriately, in 1972, marked an uneasy and none too effective attempt to transpose the Dracula legend from 19th-century Transylvania to the swinging Chelsea of London in 1972. The script never gelled but there was good news for all devotees of the Vampire movie—Peter Cushing was back again, and in two roles! The first, taking place on a tumultuous coach drive through the London of 1873, is a superb fight to the death with Dracula, on the roof of the coach, until Dracula is killed, impaled on the shattered spoke of one of the wheels. Only his ashes, his medallion and his signet ring are left, to be rescued by a disciple. The film then moves to modern London, where Dracula is summoned to life again through magic rites performed in the desanctified church of St. Botolph's by Johnny Alucard. Lee claims his first victim, an all too willing Caroline Munro, before going on his contemporary ravage through the city. Cushing as Van Helsing is brought back into the fight against the Vampire by his granddaughter Jessica (Stephanie Beacham) and Scotland Yard in the shape of Inspector Murray (Michael Coles). Cushing and Lee, apart from their first battle, are indifferently used by director Alan Gibson, but nonetheless give considerably more to the film than it in reality contains, although Van Helsing finds that not all is well in the realms of 20th-century Vampire-killing. He discovers that, as he says: "Garlic is not 100 per cent effective," and he despatches Lee with a deluge of holy water.

Lee's final—to date—appearance as the Count was in *The Satanic Rites of Dracula* in 1973, again directed by Alan Gibson for Hammer. This time the film is a mixture of motorcycle gangs, black magic, big business and cellars filled with female Vampires, and while it is somewhat better than *Dracula A.D. 1972* in integrating Dracula into modern London and establishing some gothic atmosphere, it still represents a continuing decline from the high standards set by Terence Fisher's *Dracula* in 1958. Lee is suitably impressive both as the property millionaire D. D. Denham, and, when unmasked, as the snarling Count himself. Cushing acquits himself as admirably as ever in the part of Van Helsing, this time called into battle not only by his old friend, Inspector Murray of Scotland Yard, but also at the request of Colonel Mathews, head of the Secret Service Department, S.I.7! But the concept of Count Dracula sponsoring a deadly bacterial research programme aimed at world domination, "mod" motorcycling gangs as protection for the Vampire, and black magic never settle into a unity, and the film literally ends on a dying fall. Dracula, in hot pursuit of Van Helsing, who has already failed to kill him with the traditional silver bullet, stumbles and falls into the—for him—deadly embrace of a hawthorn bush.

Lee had always expressed his ambition, as he was given less in each subsequent Hammer film, to portray a Dracula more in line with the character in Stoker's book. In 1970, he made *Count Dracula* in Europe, with a screenplay by the film's producer, Harry Alan Towers writing as "Peter Welbeck". In this Lee did play Dracula as an older man and there was some fidelity to the Stoker story line, but audiences were unable to accept the be-whiskered Lee, preferring the handsome Count Dracula they had come to love and hate. The film was not released until 1973 and Jess Franco's pedestrian direction, a clearly tight budget and poor supporting cast all worked against the film's acceptance or success.

Christopher Lee as *Dracula* in 1958 had revived the role of the Vampire Count from the tomb in which it had lain for so long, and in doing so made the role uniquely his own, for as long as he wants to don cloak, fangs and, for climactic scenes, the crimson contact lenses. He combines, even in his least satisfactory movies, a grace of action and a mesmeric charm and fatal attraction to Count Dracula, while never failing to bring out the true and very real evil of the man.

A VARIETY OF VA

Vampire films have proliferated all over the world, mirroring both the legends of Vampirism in different cultures and the spread in particular of Hammer films. The genre encompasses films from such disparate sources as the U.S. and South Korea, Britain and Italy, Mexico and the Philippines.

Before the international spread of Vampire movies, the U.S. dominated the scene – until Abbott and Costello put an end to the first cycle of the screen Vampire by laying unfunny waste to Count Dracula and all the classic movie monsters in the late Forties. After *Dracula* and *Frankenstein*, Majestic Films, a minor Hollywood production company, was first past the post in 1933 when they made *The Vampire Bat* under the somewhat prosaic direction of Frank Strayer. Running for under an hour, the movie got by mainly because of its top line cast, with villain Lionel Atwill using the fear of Vampirism to terrify the townspeople in his crazed search for "blood substitute". Ace screamer Fay Wray flexed her lungs and vocal cords and the romantic lead was Melvyn Douglas, fresh from his horror encounter with Boris Karloff in *The Old Dark House*.

Edward Van Sloan was back again as Van Helsing, the tireless Vampire Killer, in 1936 for Universal's sequel to Lugosi's *Dracula*, *Dracula's Daughter*, the first of many daughters and brides of the more famous and successful movie monsters. English-born Gloria Holden looked a suitably high-cheekboned lady Vampire in the title. She is the object of Van Helsing's search as he exclaims: "We must find it and destroy it!", although he was not to be her nemesis this time. It is her jealous

servant and lover, Sandor, played by Irving Pichel who despatches her.

Gloria Holden plays Countess Marya Zaleska who comes to England and Carfax Abbey to claim the body of her dead father, the Count himself. Later, in one of the movie's best scenes, she consigns his body to the flames and then entices his killers back to Transylvania to obtain her revenge. However, like many female vampires to follow, she prefers the idea of "normal" wedded bliss to the perverse delights of the Living Dead and so perishes as she protects the very mortal Otto Kruger from Sandor's arrow. The still unfulfilled Van Sloan speaks her epitaph: "She was beautiful when she died – 100 years ago!"

Also in 1936, Lambert Hillyer, who having cut his horror teeth with Karloff and Lugosi in Universal's *The Invisible Ray*, directed *Dracula's Daughter* from Garrett Fort's script at a cracking pace. *Dracula's Daughter* is effective horror with a pervasive atmosphere of abnormal sexuality, especially in those scenes where Countess Marya Zaleska claims her female victims, Marguerite Churchill and Nan Gray.

The Return of Dr X saw Humphrey Bogart sentenced to "B" pictures to play the white-faced executed child murderer, Maurice Xavier, complete with a white streak in his hair, brought back to life and seeking a constant supply of human blood to keep him alive! Bogart was the main point of interest in the movie, leading him to remark to an interviewer, apropos his then employers, the Warner brothers: "This was one of the pictures that made me march in to Jack Warner and ask for more money again. You can't believe what this one

Vampire films have proliferated all over the world, mirroring both the legends of Vampirism in different cultures and the spread in particular of Hammer films. The genre encompasses films from such disparate sources as the U.S. and South Korea, Britain and Italy, Mexico and the Philippines.

Before the international spread of Vampire movies, the U.S. dominated the scene – until Abbott and Costello put an end to the first cycle of the screen Vampire by laying unfunny waste to Count Dracula and all the classic movie monsters in the late Forties. After *Dracula* and *Frankenstein*, Majestic Films, a minor Hollywood production company, was first past the post in 1933 when they made *The Vampire Bat* under the somewhat prosaic direction of Frank Strayer. Running for under an hour, the movie got by mainly because of its top line cast, with villain Lionel Atwill using the fear of Vampirism to terrify the townspeople in his crazed search for "blood substitute". Ace screamer Fay Wray flexed her lungs and vocal cords and the romantic lead was Melvyn Douglas, fresh from his horror encounter with Boris Karloff in *The Old Dark House*.

Edward Van Sloan was back again as Van Helsing, the tireless Vampire Killer, in 1936 for Universal's sequel to Lugosi's *Dracula*, *Dracula's Daughter*, the first of many daughters and brides of the more famous and successful movie monsters. English-born Gloria Holden looked a suitably high-cheekboned lady Vampire in the title. She is the object of Van Helsing's search as he exclaims: "We must find it and destroy it!", although he was not to be her nemesis this time. It is her jealous

servant and lover, Sandor, played by Irving Pichel who despatches her.

Gloria Holden plays Countess Marya Zaleska who comes to England and Carfax Abbey to claim the body of her dead father, the Count himself. Later, in one of the movie's best scenes, she consigns his body to the flames and then entices his killers back to Transylvania to obtain her revenge. However, like many female vampires to follow, she prefers the idea of "normal" wedded bliss to the perverse delights of the Living Dead and so perishes as she protects the very mortal Otto Kruger from Sandor's arrow. The still unfulfilled Van Sloan speaks her epitaph: "She was beautiful when she died – 100 years ago!"

Also in 1936, Lambert Hillyer, who having cut his horror teeth with Karloff and Lugosi in Universal's *The Invisible Ray*, directed *Dracula's Daughter* from Garrett Fort's script at a cracking pace. *Dracula's Daughter* is effective horror with a pervasive atmosphere of abnormal sexuality, especially in those scenes where Countess Marya Zaleska claims her female victims, Marguerite Churchill and Nan Gray.

The Return of Dr X saw Humphrey Bogart sentenced to "B" pictures to play the white-faced executed child murderer, Maurice Xavier, complete with a white streak in his hair, brought back to life and seeking a constant supply of human blood to keep him alive! Bogart was the main point of interest in the movie, leading him to remark to an interviewer, apropos his then employers, the Warner brothers: "This was one of the pictures that made me march in to Jack Warner and ask for more money again. You can't believe what this one

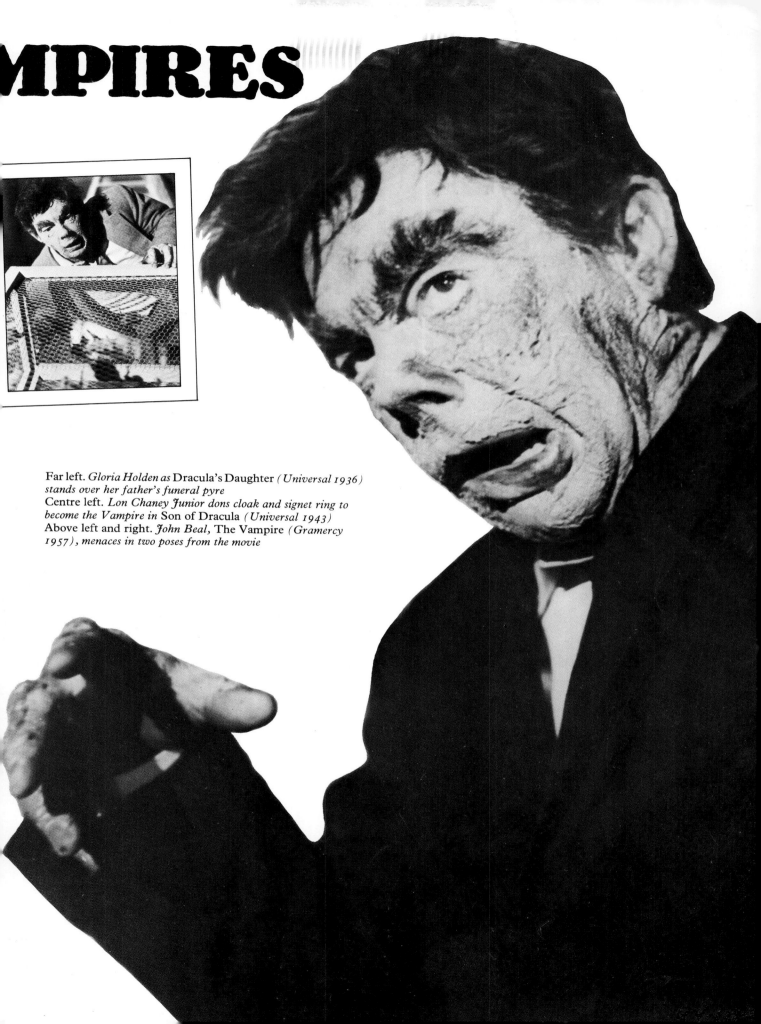

Far left. *Gloria Holden as* Dracula's Daughter *(Universal 1936)
stands over her father's funeral pyre*
Centre left. *Lon Chaney Junior dons cloak and signet ring to
become the Vampire in* Son of Dracula *(Universal 1943)*
Above left and right. *John Beal*, The Vampire *(Gramercy
1957), menaces in two poses from the movie*

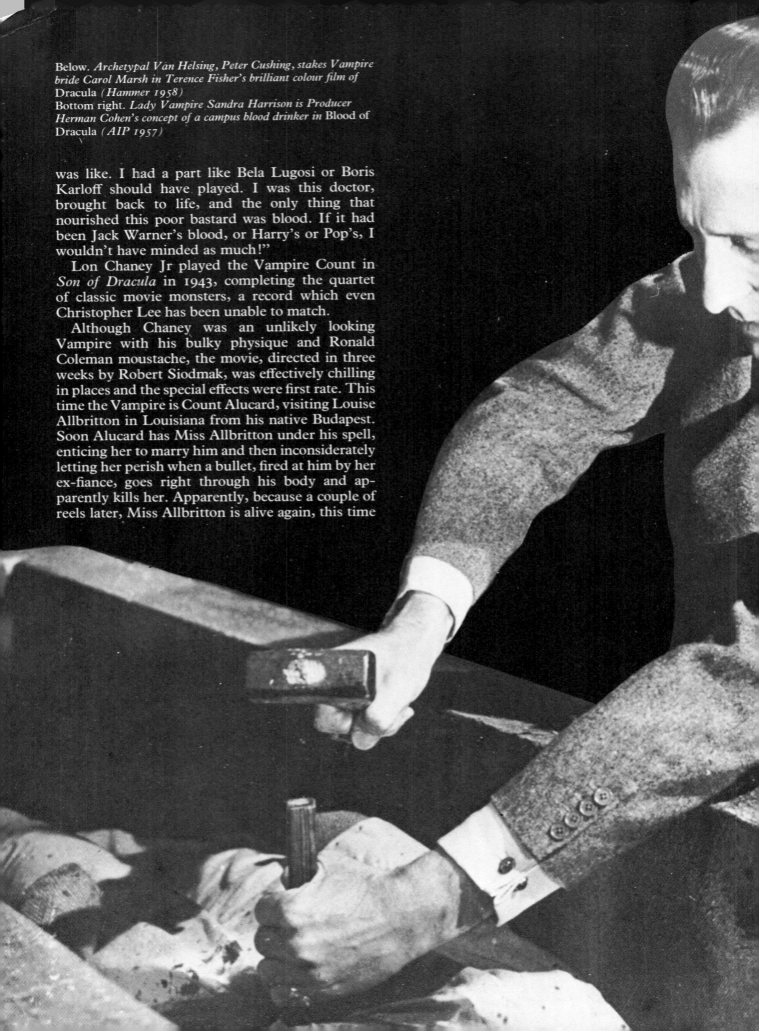

Below. *Archetypal Van Helsing, Peter Cushing, stakes Vampire bride Carol Marsh in Terence Fisher's brilliant colour film of* Dracula *(Hammer 1958)*
Bottom right. *Lady Vampire Sandra Harrison is Producer Herman Cohen's concept of a campus blood drinker in* Blood of Dracula *(AIP 1957)*

was like. I had a part like Bela Lugosi or Boris Karloff should have played. I was this doctor, brought back to life, and the only thing that nourished this poor bastard was blood. If it had been Jack Warner's blood, or Harry's or Pop's, I wouldn't have minded as much!"

Lon Chaney Jr played the Vampire Count in *Son of Dracula* in 1943, completing the quartet of classic movie monsters, a record which even Christopher Lee has been unable to match.

Although Chaney was an unlikely looking Vampire with his bulky physique and Ronald Coleman moustache, the movie, directed in three weeks by Robert Siodmak, was effectively chilling in places and the special effects were first rate. This time the Vampire is Count Alucard, visiting Louise Allbritton in Louisiana from his native Budapest. Soon Alucard has Miss Allbritton under his spell, enticing her to marry him and then inconsiderately letting her perish when a bullet, fired at him by her ex-fiance, goes right through his body and apparently kills her. Apparently, because a couple of reels later, Miss Allbritton is alive again, this time

as a Vampire, luring her ex-fiance out of jail with promises of immortality. However, hero Robert Paige is able to resist the Vampire's blandishments and, after a struggle in which the Count is able to pick him up and hurl him through the scenery, he finds Alucard's coffin in a storm drain and destroys it. Unable to return to his coffin by sun-up, Alucard perishes. He never really had a chance, relying as he did on spelling his name backwards to maintain his anonymity!

Universal filmed the first of their multi-monster movies in 1944, and John Carradine, a tall, gaunt ex-Shakespearean actor, donned top hat, white tie and cloak for the first time in *House of Frankenstein*. Erle C. Kenton put together the Frankenstein creature (played by Glenn Strange), the Wolf Man (Lon Chaney Jr), J. Carroll Naish as a psychopathic hunchback, Boris Karloff as jailbird mad scientist Dr Gustav Niemann, and Carradine in the role of Count Dracula. Writers Edward T. Lowe and Curt Siodmak had included the Mummy as well at one point in pre-production but presumably Universal make-up wizard Jack Pierce felt that Chaney's yak hairs and Strange's monster make-up were sufficient work for one movie!

Carradine was back as Vampire Count Latos in *House of Dracula* in 1945, with the same director as his previous movie, Erle C. Kenton, and Lon Chaney Jr and Glenn Strange. This time Dr Edelmann (Onslow Stevens) has a go at bringing the Count back to life but the transfusion is a mess, infecting the Doctor with the curse of the Vampire as well. The Doctor finally destroys Carradine,

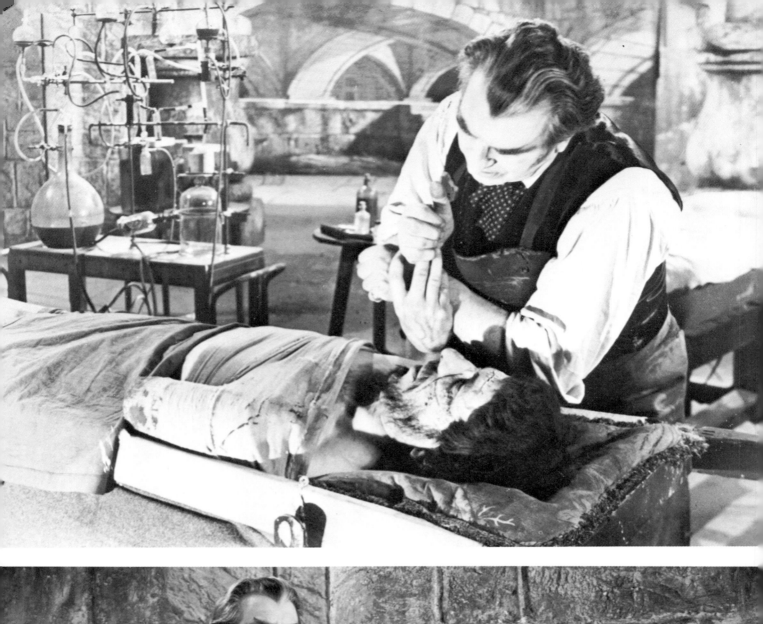

preventing him just in time from vampirizing pretty Jane Adams. He is himself destroyed as a Vampire by, of all people, Lon Chaney Jr's Lawrence Talbot!

Dracula's place in the cinema was made even more certain in 1945 when he appeared as a cartoon character, this time in *Mighty Mouse Meets Bad Bill Bunion*. The temporary slide of the genre into the realm of the "B" feature was confirmed in 1945 with *The Vampire's Ghost*, which had the Vampire loose in West Africa in a farrago that added nothing to the cycle. Next in line was John Beal in 1957's *The Vampire* in which he becomes a Vampire as a result of his addiction to pills—in this case, becoming hooked after accidentally taking pills from a bottle bequeathed to him by a researcher into Vampire bats.

The female Vampire reappeared fully fanged in the widow-peaked form of campus blood-drinker Sandra Harrison in *Blood of Dracula* in 1957. Under the hypnotic command of College Tutor Louise Lewis, Sandra emerged from the stable of Producer Herman Cohen that provided other teenage monsters in *I was a Teenage Frankenstein* and *I Was a Teenage Werewolf*. The film, aimed at the lucrative youth market in America, made a killing at the box-office, even if its on-screen Vampire carnage did not live up to the claim: "In her eyes, DESIRE! In her veins the blood of a . . . MONSTER!"

Dracula came back twice in 1958, once and authoritatively, when Christopher Lee took the title role in Terence Fisher's *Dracula* and, less impressively, in *The Return of Dracula* in which Francis Lederer was Count Bellac, Vampire refugee in the United States. In Britain, Jimmy Sangster took time off from Hammer to write the screenplay of *Blood of The Vampire*, directed as a Hammer look-alike by Henry Cass in vivid and gory Eastman Colour. Sir Donald Wolfit played sadistic revived Vampire Doctor Callistratus in the barnstorming manner of an actor playing to an audience composed exclusively of the hard of hearing, destroying any credibility the film might have had.

Curse of The Undead showed a new twist to the Vampire legend, with Australian Michael Pate as Drake Robey, the most effective, if not the fastest, gun in the West. He could not be bested in gun-fights because, quite simply, he was Undead Vampire Don Drago Robles. Only a bullet tipped with a piece of the True Cross by the local priest

finally put paid to him in the 1959 movie. Roger Corman added his own variation to the theme of the blood drinker with his *The Little Shop of Horrors* in 1960. This zestful piece was shot in the record time of two days! The Vampire in this case was a man-eating plant developed by Seymour Krelboind (Jonathan Haze) which suddenly flourishes when sprinkled with blood from one of his fingers. The Vampiristic plant is soon insatiable, demanding food which Krelboind has to obtain by murder. The ungrateful plant appears not to appreciate these ministrations, unfortunately opening its blossoms to the police to display the reflected faces of its victims!

1960 also saw the real re-emergence of the female of the species with Terence Fisher's *Brides of Dracula*, Hammer Films' sequel to the Christopher Lee *Dracula* and Roger Vadim's *Blood and Roses (Et Mourir de Plaisir)*, with his new wife Annette Stroyberg as the Vampire lead. The film was yet another adaptation of Le Fanu's *Carmilla*, but although full frontal lesbian Vampirism burst onto the screen, impeccably photographed by master cinematographer Claude Renoir, Vadim made a botch of the movie.

Fisher's film *Brides of Dracula* is another matter altogether. It is one of those movies, so perfectly put in context that they remain untouched either by the passage of time or changes in censorship codes. Fisher was able, without any of the crudity or nudity employed in *Blood and Roses*, to make quite explicit the lesbian sexuality and perversion of his female vampires, and added yet another frisson when the Vampire's mother, Baroness Meinster, played beautifully by Martita Hunt, becomes a Vampire herself, after an incestuous attack by her son. In a scene that combines genuine horror with pathos, the Baroness nervous as a newly-married bride twitches her veil away from her face to display the fangs of the Vampire.

Italy was responsible for the sword-and-sandal entry in the Vampire stakes with *Maciste Contro il Vampiro (Goliath and The Vampires)* with ex-Tarzan Gordon Scott as Goliath and Guido Celano as Kobrak the Vampire. The latter, dressed strangely in black plastic and a fright wig, pops on and off screen, demands a shipload of virgins and other goodies before being killed by Goliath.

1963 saw Boris Karloff making his one and only screen appearance as a Vampire in the omnibus Italian movie *Tre Volti Della Paura (Black*

41

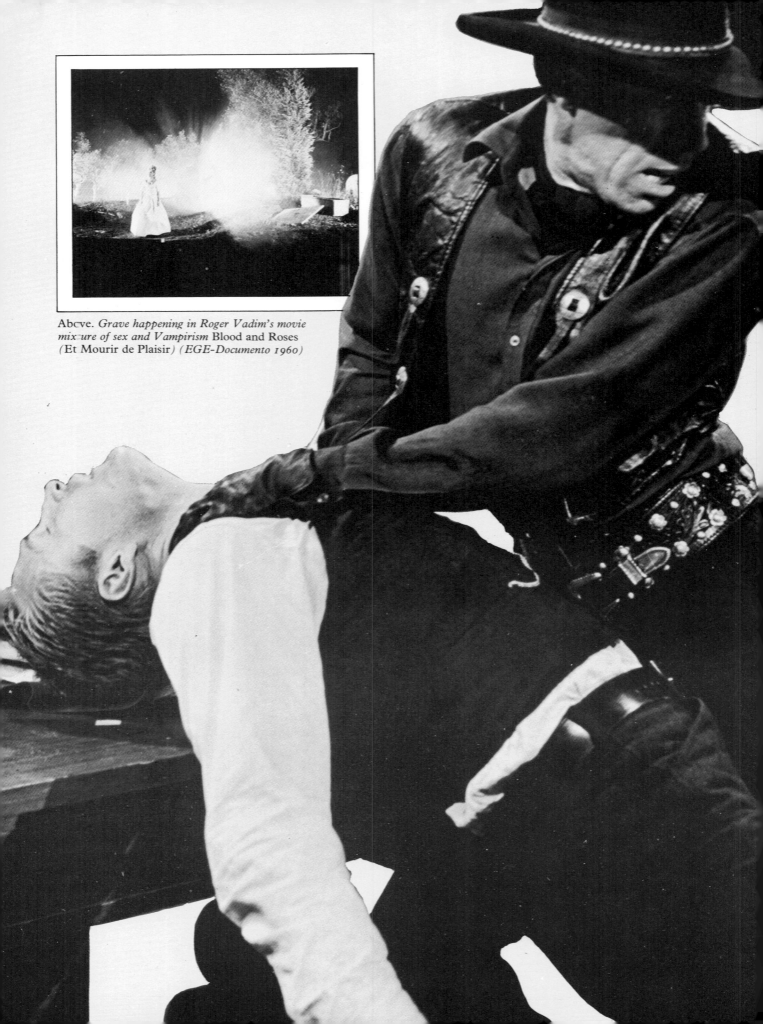

Abcve. *Grave happening in Roger Vadim's movie mix-ure of sex and Vampirism* Blood and Roses (Et Mourir de Plaisir) *(EGE-Documento 1960)*

Left. Way out West, Eric Fleming nearly falls victim to Vampire gunfighter Michael Pate in Curse of The Undead *(Universal 1959)*
Right. David Peel as Vampire Baron Meinster decays from the Holy Water thrown over him by Peter Cushing in Terence Fisher's Brides of Dracula *(Hammer 1960)*

Sabbath). Karloff spoke the narration that linked the three stories and appeared in *The Wurdalak*, from a story by Tolstoy, in which he played Gorca, a type of Vampire compelled to kill its closest relatives. Despite uninteresting direction from ex-cameraman Mario Bava, Karloff is splendid, red of eye and shaggy of looks, outacting everyone in sight.

Vincent Price played a victim of the Vampire in the first version of Richard Matheson's award winning story, *I Am Legend*, in 1964's American-Italian co-production, *The Last Man on Earth*. As Chemist Robert Morgan, Price is alone in a world turned Vampire by a wind-borne plague. The production was a low budget one and despite Price's usual good performance, there is not a great charge of horror, although the movie's ending is suitably ironic. The story was strong enough, however, for it to be remade in 1971 with Charlton Heston in the title role as *The Omega Man*, alone in a Los Angeles decimated by a Sino-Russian germ war in 1977. Only the scenes of a deserted garbage-littered city and the prowling Vampires really chilled.

The female of the Vampire species is often a victim of the male Vampire, before striking out on her own to create her own carnage. Thus, in Don Sharp's *Kiss of The Vampire* in 1964, in which Noel Willman took over the Dracula role and Clifford Evans became Vampire Killer Professor Zimmer, the heroine Marianne (Jennifer Daniel)

Below. In The Omega Man, *the second filming of Richard Matheson's major novel, Charlton Heston discovers plague victims in Vampire-infested Los Angeles*

Below. *Moroccan Vampire Terence de Marney eyes a potential victim in Fredric Goode's* Hand of Night *(Pathe 1966)*
Right. *In the same movie, horrified William Sylvester finds out that the contents of the Coffin are not always what they seem to be!*

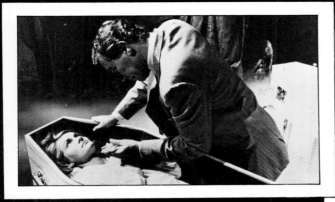

becomes a Vampire from the bite of Count Ravna. At the end of the film avenging bats take care of him, and a number of other decorative lady Vampires, including the delectable Isobel Black!

1964 also saw a female Vampire in her own right in the shapely form of Jennifer Jayne in the *VAMPIRE* episode of Freddie Francis' multi-story *Doctor Terror's House of Horrors*. Donald Sutherland finds himself married to Vampire Nicole (Jennifer Jayne) and, not surprisingly, seeks the advice of the local doctor, Max Adrian. The advice which Sutherland receives is also unexceptional—he is told that he must drive a wooden stake through his wife's heart. This Sutherland does but when the police come and

accuse him of murder, Max Adrian, an epicene villain if ever there was one, refuses to confirm his story. Sutherland is taken away to jail while Adrian, reflecting that "There isn't enough room in this town for *two* Vampires!", turns into a bat and flies out of the window!

1965 saw John Carradine triumphantly back as the Vampire Count in the splendidly awful *Billy The Kid vs Dracula*. Among the activities which the Count gets up to in the West is his unfortunate attack upon an Indian squaw during a stopover on a stage-coach journey. This leads to a full-blooded Indian attack on the stage and its passengers, from which Dracula escapes to go on to the town of Wickenberg where he stays with

Below. *Vampire acolyte dies by the bat in Don Sharp's* Kiss of Evil *(Hammer 1962)*

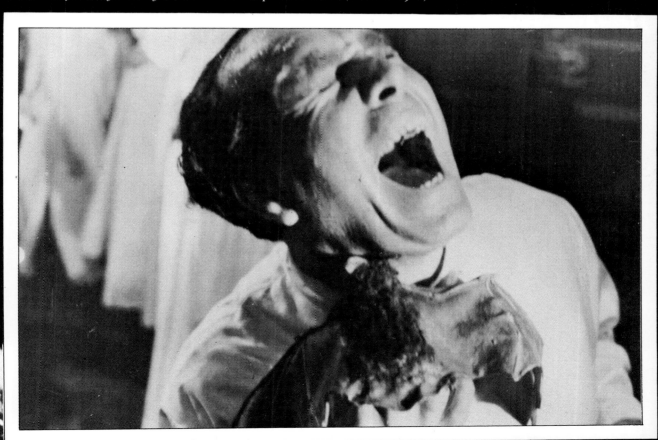

Above. *Peter Cushing kills Ingrid Pitt in* The Vampire Lovers *(Hammer/AIP 1970)* Bottom left. *Jon Pertwee sinks his fangs into John Bennett in* The House That Dripped Blood *(Amicus 1970)* Bottom right. *Roman Polanski in his* Dance of The Vampires *(Cadre/Filmways 1967)*

Melinda Plowman (Betty Bentley). The heroine's ranch is managed by retired gunslinger Billy the Kid (Chuck Courtney) who, after Melinda is vampirized by Carradine, tracks him to a mine and drives a stake through his heart. As Carradine goes back to dust once more, Melinda awakes from her Vampire trance. John Carradine is as gaunt and zestful as ever back in his cloak and the whole movie moves along at a cracking pace, well directed by William Beaudine.

Christopher Lee was Phillipe Darvas, stage director of the Theatre de Mort of Paris, and a red-herring in the tradition of Chaney before him, in the 1966 movie, *Theatre of Blood*. Not surprisingly, Lee is suspected of being responsible for a wave of Vampire killings sweeping Paris, until, somewhat inconsiderately, he is found dead long before the movie ends, leaving the real killer to be unmasked. 1966's *The Hand of Night* moved the locale quite effectively to North Africa, with Moroccan Vampires Terence de Marney, with a nice line in malformed eyes, and Alizia Gur terrorizing hero William Sylvester. Further afield still, from the

Philippines, came Ronald Remy as Marco the Vampire, one of 1966's *The Blood Drinkers*. He spreads terror and Vampirism throughout a Philippine village, including the Chief of Police, who was bitten by a corpse in the local morgue! Marco is intent upon transferring the heart from village maiden Charita into the dying body of her twin sister, his sweetheart, and director Gerardo de Leon made a quite convincing Gothic movie, filled with swirling studio fog and a fine variety of red and blue filters to accentuate the action.

In 1967, Christopher Lee returned in the German movie *Die Schlangengrube und das Pendel (The Blood Demon)* which had little in common with Poe's story, but many rather splendid echoes from other horror movies made by James Whale, Roger Corman and Mario Bava. Lee is Count Regula, executed by being hanged, drawn and quartered for the murder of a dozen virgins and brought to life again by the transfusion of green blood provided by his faithful retainer Anatol! The movie had some good chilled moments, particularly a ghostly ride through a literally dead

47

forest, with branches filled with severed limbs and torsos. There was a fine selection of animals infesting the castle and insects crawling over heroine Karin Dor. Unfortunately, there was not enough of Lee and erstwhile Tarzan Lex Barker made a wooden leading man.

1967 also saw Roman Polanski's attempt at a satire on the genre, *The Dance of The Vampires* (called *The Fearless Vampire Killers* in Britain), but despite some effective moments Polanski's film was generally unsuccessful. The art of all good satire is to know intimately the subject being satirized, and clearly Polanski did not. The script, by Gerard Brach and Polanski, often sounded as though it had not been fully translated from its original Polish, and Polanski further diluted his

attack by playing one of the Vampire killers. On the credit side, there was fine muted art direction with Wilfrid Shingleton providing a splendidly gothic and uneasy Transylvania, a surprisingly good performance from ex-boxer Terry Downs as obligatory hunchback, vanishing behind a snow-drift with a wolf, only to re-appear with a satisfied look and blood and fur on his lips, and an excellent Vampire from Ferdy Mayne. Mayne was Count Von Krolock, a suave Middle European Vampire host to seekers after the truth Polanski and Jack MacGowran, and father to a gay Vampire son (Iain Quarrier). Sharon Tate as the innkeeper's daughter bitten into Vampirism is a beautiful heroine, never less so than when snatched from the bath by Count Von Krolock, leaving only a sinister rim of blood-stained soap suds.

In 1969, *Blood of Dracula's Castle* had John Carradine, not as the Vampire Count but instead playing butler to Alex D'Arcy, known here as Count Townsend. Spending their days in twin coffins, Count and Countess Townsend dine from the blood of young girls conveniently kept chained in the cellar, having their sustenance brought to them in true style by butler Carradine, offering the repast with comments like: "I think you'll enjoy this vintage." Despite all the conveniences the Townsends end as dust, cheating the audience by not disintegrating on-screen.

1970 proved a good year for Vampire movies, in quantity if not necessarily in quality. Quite the strangest was the American *Blood of Frankenstein*, notable mainly for the last screen appearances of Lon Chaney Jr playing Groton, The Mad Zombie, and J. Carroll Naish as Doctor Frankenstein. *Creatures of Evil* were some Philippine Vampires brought to the screen by director Gerardo De Leon. They included Eddie Garcia turned into a Vampire by a bite from his mother and Amalia Fuentes as Leonora, saved from becoming one of the Undead by a crucifix driven through her heart, only to be reunited as a ghost with her ghostly sweetheart, Daniel! *Nacht der Vampire (Shadow of The Werewolf)* had a confused plot with Paul Naschy, something of a European cult horror actor, playing Waldemar, a heroic werewolf given to saving the heroine, who returned his kindness by plunging a cross into his heart, on the sound principle that only one who loves him can destroy the werewolf!

American International and Hammer combined to bring another version of *Carmilla* to the screen with *The Vampire Lovers* in 1970 in which Ingrid Pitt was the Vampire protagonist. Returning from the grave to take revenge for the deaths of her relatives, Ingrid turns her whole attention to the females of the cast, happily putting a number of bare breasts on display and Vampirizing Pippa Steel, Madeleine Smith—whose bosom companion she becomes—and the Governess, Kate O'Mara! Peter Cushing makes a guest appearance as General Spielsdorf who finally destroys Miss Pitt, not only driving a stake into her but also cutting off her head for good measure!

The pan-European 1970 *Le Rouge aux Levres (Daughters of Darkness)* had a highly improbable Delphine Seyrig as Vampire Countess Batory who, after a number of overtly lesbian scenes, ends up flying through the windscreen of a crashing car, to be inelegantly impaled on the branch of a tree! 1970's *House of Dark Shadows* took America's popular daytime television programme *Dark Shadows* and, with the original cast, beefed it up for the Big Screen. Jonathan Frid played the 18th-century Vampire Barnabas Collins, released from his coffin and loose again in 20th-century Maine. Somewhat improbably, Doctor Julia Hoffman (Grayson Hall) attempts to cure Barnabas of his Vampirism by medical means, but when her love is spurned, she reverses the process and he reverts to his true age of 175 years. Eventually he goes the

way of all Vampires, shot with a cross-bow by Roger Davis, but not before he provides a movie that is both chilling and exciting.

Robert Quarry made the first of his three appearances as American-International's Count Yorga, one of the few Vampires to fit comfortably into a contemporary setting, in Bob Kelljan's *Count Yorga, Vampire* in 1970. Set in Los Angeles, it carries a charge of horror, due to underplayed acting, to simple, unfussy direction and to good special effects from James Tannenbaum. *Incense For The Damned*, beset by production problems which took the director's name off the film, mixed sex and Vampirism in Greece with blood-drinking among the dreaming spires of Oxford. Patrick Mower wrestles with the curse of the Vampire under duress from "mental Vampire" Peter Cushing who played Oxford don, Dr Goodrich. The movie is a botched version of the book *Doctors Wear Scarlet*, but the performances of Cushing and Patrick Macnee, and of guest star Edward Woodward as Vampire expert Holmstrom who happily confirmed for the shocked Alex Davion that the drinking of blood can definitely give sexual pleasure, are excellent.

1971 saw Peter Duffell's superb multi-story movie for Amicus, *The House That Dripped Blood*. In the episode "The Cloak", Jon Pertwee played Paul Henderson, star of countless horror movies, who, disgusted by the cheapness of his current opus, buys himself a new cloak from strange second-hand dealer Geoffrey Bayldon. Unknowingly, Henderson has purchased a real Vampire's cloak and soon finds himself levitating at midnight. Rising from his coffin to wrestle with an avenging Inspector Holloway (John Bennett) a stake is driven through his heart. In one of the few really good horror movie spoofs, Duffell brilliantly manages both the humour and the horror.

Jimmy Sangster, who had written the screenplay for Christopher Lee's *Dracula* in 1958, returned to the genre as director with *Lust For a Vampire* in 1971. This had Yutte Stensgaard as the Vampire, Mircalla, revived from a skeleton when the Countess, Barbara Jefford, pours blood on it from a golden chalice, freshly filled at the cut throat of a sacrificed peasant girl. Soon she is exerting her influence over the pupils of the Exclusive Finishing School For Young Ladies which is using the castle that was once the home of the Undead Karnsteins. Finally the villagers set

Above. *The end of Vampire Wanda Ventham in Brian Clemens'* Captain Kronos – Vampire Hunter *(Hammer 1972)*
Inset. *Andy Warhol's concept of the Vampire infects the screen with Udo Kier as The Count in Paul Morissey's* Blood for Dracula *(Compagnia Cinematografica Champion (Rome)/Jean Yanne 1973)*

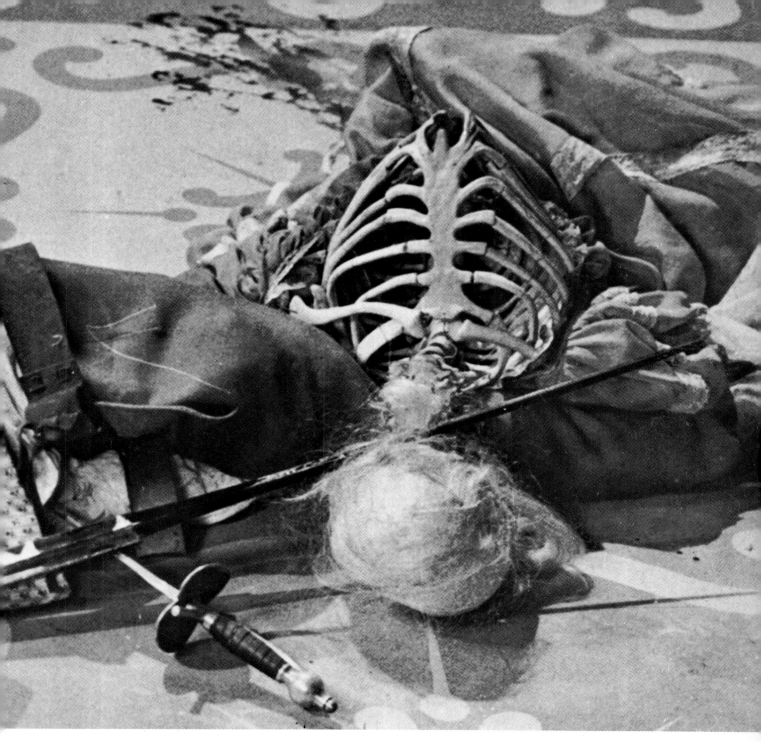

fire to Karnstein Castle and a falling beam, still blazing, crashes down conveniently to pierce the Vampire's heart. Horror and sexuality is well to the fore, and Sangster is able to pace the lesbian encounters well, although the film falls to bits towards the end, in a succession of plot turns and Vampire attacks.

1971 was a good year for the Hammer Vampire, with Peter Sasdy bringing Ingrid Pitt onto the screen in Jeremy Paul's version of the Countess Batory legend, *Countess Dracula*. Ingrid keeps herself young and beautiful and alive by constant bathing in the blood of young virgins, murdering a continuing number of girls to keep her bath well

filled. But she still finds time to court Imre (Sandor Eles), a young Hungarian Hussar. After she kills her daughter Ilona (Lesley-Anne Down), thereby depriving herself of rejuvenating blood, her face crumbles into hideous senility.

Also in 1971, John Hough directed *Twins of Evil* with Peter Cushing as fanatical witch- and vampire-burning Gustav Weil. The Vampire Count Karnstein is played by Damien Thomas and the title roles taken by the twins Mary and Madeleine Collinson. The foolish Karnstein reincarnates his Vampire ancestor, Countess Mircalla (Katya Wyeth), the first of the film's Vampires, as he stabs a girl strapped to Mircalla's tomb! Soon he

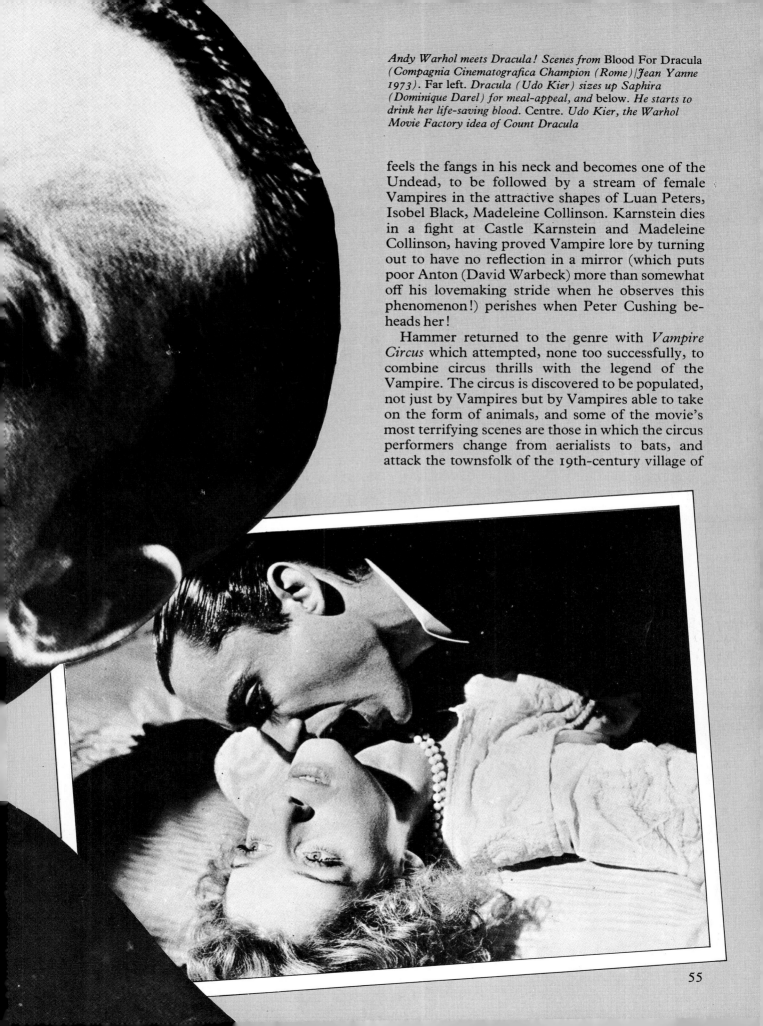

Andy Warhol meets Dracula! Scenes from Blood For Dracula *(Compagnia Cinematografica Champion (Rome)/Jean Yanne 1973).* Far left. *Dracula (Udo Kier) sizes up Saphira (Dominique Darel) for meal-appeal, and* below. *He starts to drink her life-saving blood.* Centre. *Udo Kier, the Warhol Movie Factory idea of Count Dracula*

feels the fangs in his neck and becomes one of the Undead, to be followed by a stream of female Vampires in the attractive shapes of Luan Peters, Isobel Black, Madeleine Collinson. Karnstein dies in a fight at Castle Karnstein and Madeleine Collinson, having proved Vampire lore by turning out to have no reflection in a mirror (which puts poor Anton (David Warbeck) more than somewhat off his lovemaking stride when he observes this phenomenon!) perishes when Peter Cushing beheads her!

Hammer returned to the genre with *Vampire Circus* which attempted, none too successfully, to combine circus thrills with the legend of the Vampire. The circus is discovered to be populated, not just by Vampires but by Vampires able to take on the form of animals, and some of the movie's most terrifying scenes are those in which the circus performers change from aerialists to bats, and attack the townsfolk of the 19th-century village of

himself involved in a preposterous plot of out-of-space invaders on Earth to use bodies of dead scientists to recreate the monsters of terror, Dracula, The Werewolf, The Mummy and Frankenstein's Creature! Apart from having to lead the aliens in their nefarious activities, Michael Rennie is further imposed upon by having to share the movie with Continental horror favourite, Paul Naschy, an actor with serious limitations as a performer.

1972 brought France's Alain Delon into the genre with his role as Doctor Devilers in Alain Jessua's *Traitment de Choc* which was given the catchpenny title of *Doctor in The Nude* in England. This highly entertaining movie had Delon using the blood and organs of Portuguese boys at his clinic in a modern-day Vampire treatment of injections to revive his tired patients! Also in 1972, Mike Raven made a good stab at the role of the 18th-century Vampire, *Grave of The Vampire*. Michael Pataki was Caleb Croft, a particularly unpleasant Vampire who fathers an unpleasant son after raping Leslie (Kitty Vallacher) in an open grave and killing her

Schtettel. Robert Tayman made a good Vampire Count, ending up decapitated by John Moulder Brown, but neither actor was able to exorcise memories of Hammer's Christopher Lee and Peter Cushing in their archetypal roles of Vampire and Vampire-killer, and director Robert Young had neither the authority nor the feeling for the genre adequately to be able to weld the film's disparate elements.

In *El Hombre que Vino de Ummo (Dracula versus Frankenstein)* in 1971, Michael Rennie finds

boyfriend Paul when they had most unwisely left a college party to make love in a cemetery!

William Marshall made his first movie appearance to cash in with the then box-office success of Black movies in the United States by portraying the first Black Vampire in 1972's *Blacula*. Under William Crain's direction, Blacula is made a Vampire by Count Dracula (Charles Macaulay) in hopes of getting the Count's support in his crusade to end the slave trade. Unsuccessful in that, he surfaces more than 150 years later in Los Angeles, revived by two gay interior decorators who had looted his castle in search of objets d'art. Appropriately, they become Blacula's first victims. Finding the image of his lost love, in the shapely form of Vonetta McGee, Blacula seduces her. His failure to register on photographs, and the mounting number of Vampire victims in California, sets in motion the final hunt for the Vampire, which ends with Vonetta McGee staked and Blacula immolating himself in the sunlight, his love gone. You can't keep a good Vampire down, however, and Marshall was back in his fangs and cloak for 1973's *Scream, Blacula, Scream*. He is revived from a (literal) bag of bones by voodoo man Willis (Richard Lawson). This time, after biting his requisite number of victims, Blacula perishes when Lisa (Pam Grier) drives a stake through a doll replica of him.

Hammer introduced a new version of the Vampire legend with the delayed *Captain Kronos–Vampire Hunter*, but something had gone out of the once successful Hammer formula. The movie was an uneasy blend of styles, written and directed by Brian Clemens, creator of television's *The Avengers*, and chronicled the adventures of professional

Left. *The Dead rise again in Roy Ward Baker's Hong Kong filmed* The Legend of The Seven Golden Vampires
Below. *The attack of a Chinese Vampire from the same movie (Hammer/Shaw Brothers 1974)*

Vampire hunters Captain Kronos (Horst Janson) and hunchback assistant Professor Heironymous Grost (John Cater) in the fight to free the village of Durward from the scourge of the Vampire. The film gains some momentum with the attempts of Kronos to put infected doctor Marcus (John Carson) out of his misery, only finally to have the doctor killed by the steel cross around his neck, and the death of Vampire Lady Durward (Wanda Ventham) with Kronos' blessed sword.

Roy Ward Baker directed *Vault of Horror* in 1973 for Amicus and managed to insert quite a bit of atmosphere into producer Milton Subotsky's scenario in the segment "Midnight Mass". Rogers (Daniel Massey) traces his sister to a town where he is warned to "stay inside" when darkness comes. He murders his sister Donna (Massey's real-life sister, Anna) and then repairs to a nearby restaurant where he finds crowds of what turn out to be Vampires drinking real-blood Bloody Marys. Massey, in a neat end to a well-made short story, ends up as the evening's pièce-de-résistance for the Vampires, including his sister Donna—hanging upside-down with a beer tap in his neck as a supply of instant blood for the drinkers!

Paul Morrissey, under the aegis of Andy Warhol, made sure that should the Count ever rise again from the grave, Warhol and Morrissey would be his first victims. Morrissey's *Blood for Dracula*, made in 1973, had Count Dracula forced to leave his native Rumania for Italy in search of fresh supplies of virgin's blood which kept him alive. Choosing Italy as being a suitable country for the production of the raw material for his lusts, Dracula (Udo Kier) stays with the Marquis di Fiori (Vittorio De Sica) and his wife and courts the daughters of the house. They spur the Count as a suitor, repelled by his unhealthy appearance, much preferring the sexual pleasures to be found with the di Fiori's servant Mario, played by Warhol favourite, Joe Dallesandro. The film went from bad to worse with the Count being physically sick on tasting the blood of a daughter claimed to be virginal. This time the Count meets his nemesis, as might be expected from Warhol, only after he has been systematically hacked to bloody pieces with an axe by Joe Dallesandro. The whole movie is dire, with De Sica looking permanently ill at ease and a negative appearance as a "belligerent peasant" by Roman Polanski.

Cushing came back again in 1974 to restore some of the dignity to the Vampire movie in *The Legend of The Seven Golden Vampires*, the first Kung Fu horror movie, co-produced in Hong Kong by Hammer's Michael Carreras and the Shaw Brothers' Run Run Shaw. Unfortunately, Don Houghton's script never made the fusion of Kung Fu Martial Arts and the Vampire loose in the Chunking of 1904, with Cushing's Van Helsing tracking down the Seven Golden Vampires through the Chinese hinterland. The first appearance of the Undead, scrabbling up through the earth covering their graves, and advancing upon their victims in slow motion, seems to have been borrowed by director Roy Ward Baker from Hammer's *Plague of The Zombies* where John Gilling used a similar technique in the raising of the zombies. It worked well the first time, but was less effective with repetition. The fights between the Vampire killers and the monsters become somewhat monotonous, although Cushing, superb as ever in the role he has made very much his own, wielded a powerful burning torch, despatching a good number of the Undead! Baker seemed thrown, however, by the locale and some of the scenes went for nothing because of poor staging. The Dracula of John Forbes-Robertson, using the body of his disciple to infect China, is a poor substitute for Christopher Lee, and his make-up with blue lips and strange lighting make him nearer a Pantomime King than the Prince of the Vampires.

Finally, the latest, and least likely performer to don cape and fangs was David Niven in Clive Donner's 1974 *Vampira*. The movie was yet another disastrous attempt at a send-up of Vampire films, and neither Niven nor Donner was able to make much headway with Jeremy Lloyd's leaden script. This had Niven, as Count Dracula, seeking a rare blood group among the female visitors to his castle, lured there for photographic sessions for *Playboy* magazine, to revive his wife, Vampira (Teresa Graves). Unfortunately for Niven, the first transfusion turned the Countess from White to Black, forcing Dracula and his manservant to leave Transylvania for London, in order to track down the girls and remedy the error. Dracula did not even get the dignity of a traditional despatch in Lloyd's script, ending up bitten by Vampira and himself turned to a Black.

Certainly, with *Vampira*, the genre seems in something of a becalmed state, but there is sufficient blood in the movie Vampire for us to be very certain that the years to come will bring us an even better and bigger variety of Vampires.

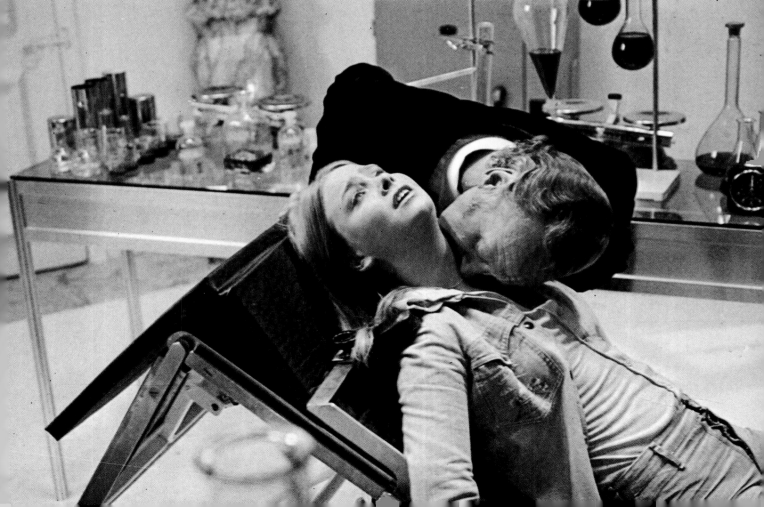

*Peter Cushing, the definitive Baron, shows Shane Briant and
Madeline Smith how to make a Monster in Hammer style in
Terence Fisher's superbly Gothic* Frankenstein And the Monster
From Hell *(Hammer 1973)*

HOW TO MAK

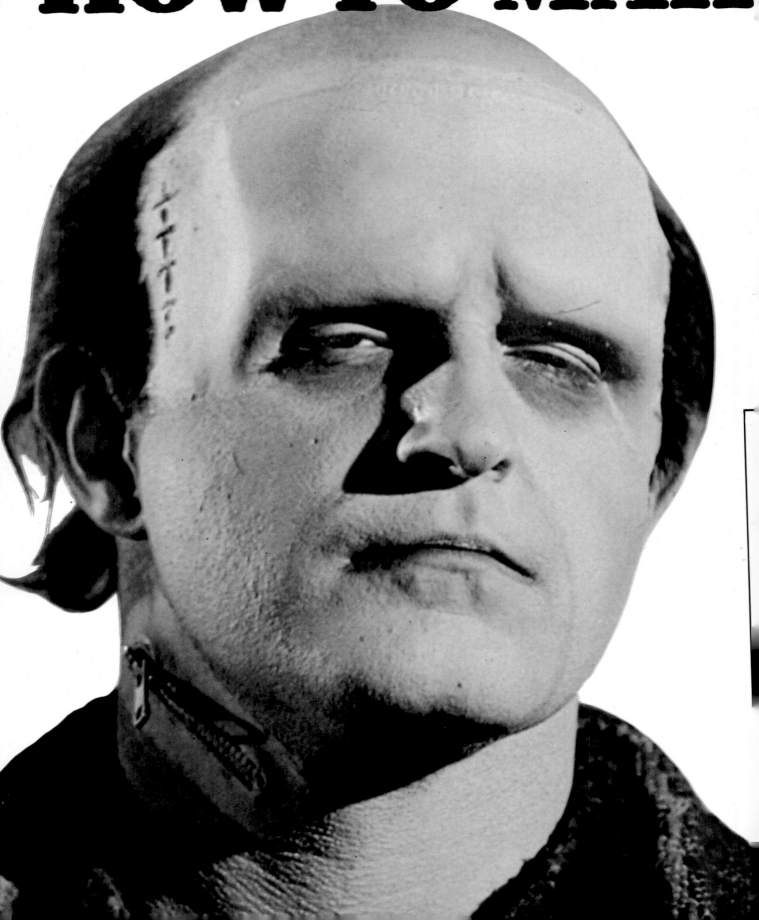

E A MONSTER

Monster-making has been a popular pastime in the cinema since Méliès and other early film-makers discovered that the camera could be made to lie most convincingly. The first "trick" films paved the way for the creation of many weird and terrible screen monsters and for shock effects far beyond the normal experiences of audiences.

The first man-made monster was created by a doctor's injection which turned man into ape in the 1908 movie *The Doctor's Experiment, or, Reversing Darwin's Theory*. Nothing deterred, when he found that the apes were there to stay, the doctor made the best of an unfortunate thing by putting the results of his experiments on public view, thus establishing a pattern of the horror film which was to see steadfast service in the years to come.

Movies' most filmed monster was nameless, the improbable creation of Mary Shelley, who published *Frankenstein : or The Modern Prometheus* in 1816, when she was still in her early 20s. In Thomas Edison's 1910 movie *Frankenstein*, the monster was played by a member of the Edison Stock Company of actors, one Charles Ogle. He appeared in his own make-up, wearing rotting bandages, a wild expression and disarranged hair.

German star Paul Wegener had first come across the legend of the Golem, a man made of clay and then brought to life to fight for the oppressed Jews, when he was filming *The Student of Prague* in 1913. Wegener was so fascinated by the story that he returned in film to it no less than three times, on each occasion playing the giant creature himself. In 1914, he co-directed *The Golem* with Henrik Galeen (who was later to write *Nosferatu*), and Galeen too took a role in the film. The Golem is discovered by workmen digging on the site of an old

Left. Peter Boyle as the zipper-necked Monster from Young Frankenstein *(Gruskoff/Venture Films/Crossbow Productions/Jouer 1974). Below. Boris Karloff menaces Mae Clarke in James Whale's* Frankenstein *(Universal 1931)*

Making a Monkey! Gustav Von Seyffertitz in a scene from
The Wizard *(Fox 1927)*

*Boris Karloff, the finest Frankenstein Monster, in Jack Pierce's
archetypal make-up.* Frankenstein *(Universal 1931)*

synagogue and sold to an antiquarian who, with
the aid of an old book of ritual, and in what was to
be the formal style of the monster movies to come,
brings it to life. Once more it was the old and
exciting story of the man who created a monster he
was unable to control: the Golem uses its strength
for evil and, when it is not unnaturally spurned by
the antiquarian's daughter (Lydia Salmonova), it
goes on a monstrous rampage through Prague
before toppling to its death from a tower. The
lowering Grimm-like sets and low-key photography
presaged the Germanically influenced 1931
Frankenstein.

Wegener was back again and stomping his clay
havoc in order to scare a dancer, Lydia Salmonova
again, in *Der Golem und die Tanzerin (The Golem
and The Ballerina)* in 1917, and he returned once
more in 1920, still with clay wig, the doublet with
its Star of David and the great boots that were to be
repeated in the Frankenstein monster's costume,
in the best of the three movies, *Der Golem Wie er in
Die Welt Kam (The Golem: How He Came Into
The World)*. Wegener directed the film and set the

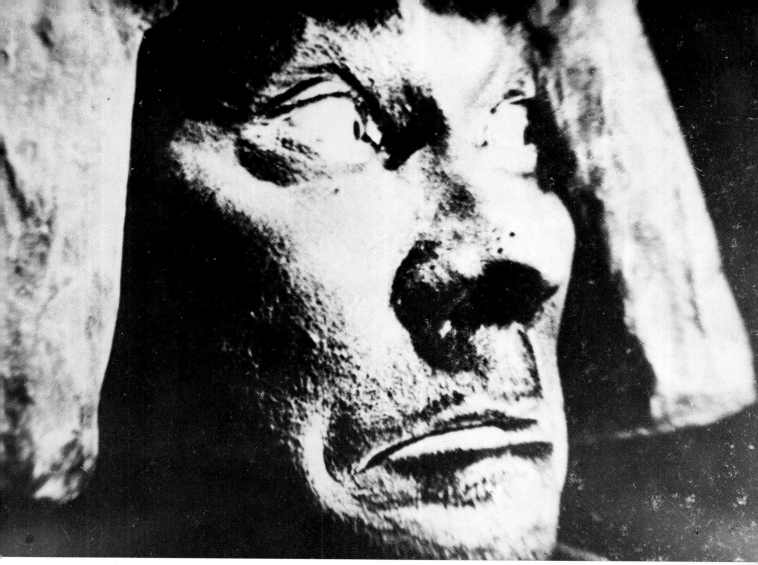

Hidden behind the mud, Paul Wegener is the Clay Man brought to life in The Golem *(Decla-Bioscop 1914)*

pattern which was in very many respects a dry run for James Whale's *Frankenstein*, sharing with that film the great cinematographer, Karl Freund. This time the film was set in its original time. Rabbi Judah Low Ben Bezalel sculpts his clay monster and then, summoning the demon Astaroth, animates him. When the Golem saves the Emperor Ludwig from death under crumbling masonry, the grateful ruler rescinds his orders for a pogrom against the Jews. But evil triumphs, for a while at any rate. The Golem is forced by the mad assistant Rabbi to kill the suitor of the Rabbi's daughter, and the creature obeys, hurling him from a tower, and sealing his own fate. After setting the tower on fire and seizing the Rabbi's daughter, the Golem smashes its terrible way through the city, only to fall, killed by a child, who unfearingly removes from its chest the mystic amulet that gave the creature life. The traditions of the horror movie were all there, from the Golem's original creation for good, to its misuse by the demented assistant, the havoc and pursuit and the final death at innocent hands.

Lon Chaney Sr entered the cinematic lists in 1922 in *A Blind Bargain*, which he made for Sam Goldwyn. In this movie, Chaney not only played the archetypal mad scientist but, as was his wont, also took the role of the hunchbacked ape-man, the horrible result of one of his experiments! Nemesis came, however, to Chaney's Dr Lamb when his alter ego set free yet another of his unsuccessful experimental results, a great simian which crushed Dr Lamb to death!

But monster-making reached a new and great peak, and created one of the greatest stars of the cinema of terror, when Boris Karloff played the creature in the Universal film of Mary Shelley's *Frankenstein* in 1931.

The studio had seen the immense popularity of *Dracula* and had rapidly realized that there was profit to be gained from horror movies. Bela Lugosi had been tested for the part of the monster but he turned it down because he had no desire to play a role without dialogue!

Universal re-assigned the directional role to Englishman James Whale who had at that time directed only two movies – *Journey's End* and

Waterloo Bridge. Whale began looking around the Universal lot to find his Creature, and, happily for the cinema, hit upon a 44-year-old bit player then making a gangster movie called *Graft*: Boris Karloff.

Whale had made drawings of Karloff's head, which, as he said, fascinated him. "His physique was weaker than I could wish, but that queer, penetrating personality of his, I felt, was more important than his shape, which could easily be altered." The final make-up and costume were created by Universal's head of make-up, Jack Pierce. The Creature, with its heavy-lidded lizard eyes, corpse-like pallor, matted hair, and, above all, the "classic" bolts in the sides of its neck, through which Dr Frankenstein would feed in the electrical power to animate it, passed into cinema history. The make-up was not enough in itself, however, to raise Karloff's monster to the levels of genius: above all, Karloff's playing, and the amazing amount of emotion he was able to convey through his eyes and the grace of his movements, raised the performance far beyond the initial curiosity and shock value.

The screenplay, written by Garrett Fort and Francis Faragoh, had Colin Clive as the obsessed Henry Frankenstein putting his Creature together from parts of corpses stolen from cemeteries with the help of his hunchbacked assistant, Fritz, played by Dwight Frye.

The creation of the monster ranks as one of the finest in screen horror. As a storm rages over the abandoned windmill in which Frankenstein is conducting his experiments, the inanimate monster, swathed in bandages, is raised on a trestle to the roof of the tower, there to receive life from the crackling electric storm. The whirring flashing laboratory equipment with its rhythmically cracking electric arc screams to a crescendo and the trestle is lowered to the floor of the laboratory once more. For what seems an eternity, nothing happens. Then, with just a twitch of its fingers, the creature moves, to Frankenstein's exultant shouts: "It's alive – it's alive – it's alive!" The most famous words in monster movies had been spoken, and Colin Clive follows these with a statement that was to be the credo of countless mad scientists to come: "Now I know what it feels like to be God!"

His triumph is short-lived, however, for the Creature, beautifully understated in its playing, is far from the perfect being Frankenstein had hoped to make. Instead, impelled by its twisted brain, the Monster is a fiend incarnate, without reason and bent only on killing. Kept chained in a dank dungeon and tormented by Fritz, the Creature finally breaks from its bonds and strangles the hunchback. Subdued once more, the monster remains incarcerated, Dr Waldman (Edward Van Sloan) having promised Frankenstein that he would destroy the ill-fated creation. Instead, on Franken-

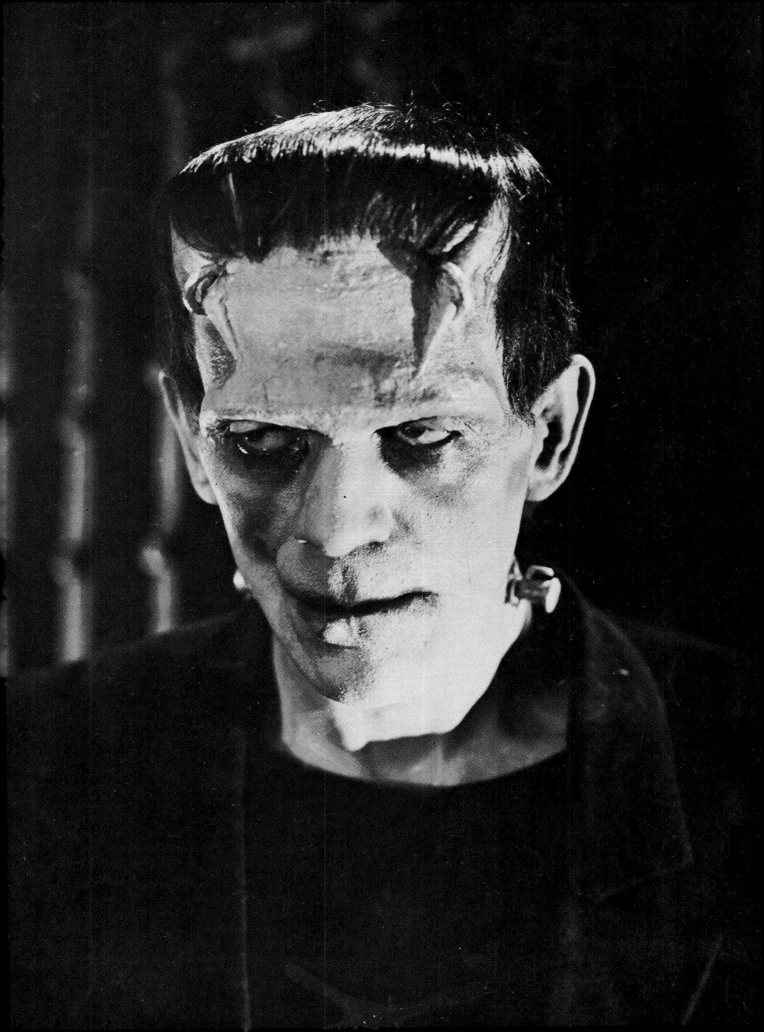

Below left. *A new Monster, Lon Chaney Junior is fitted with his bolts as he steps into Karloff's boots for* Ghost of Frankenstein *(Universal 1942), here watched in his struggles by Frankenstein scion Sir Cedric Hardwicke*
Right. *Monster and his Mate. Karloff together with Elsa Lanchester, the* Bride of Frankenstein *(Universal 1935)*

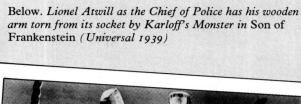

Below. *Lionel Atwill as the Chief of Police has his wooden arm torn from its socket by Karloff's Monster in* Son of Frankenstein *(Universal 1939)*

stein's wedding day, the Creature kills Waldman and escapes once more.

In the only idyllic scene in the movie, he plays with a small girl (Marilyn Harris) at the side of a lake. Here is acting of the highest calibre as Karloff, without the benefit of speech, reaches out and finds human contact with a child unafraid of his hideous appearance. Together they throw flowers onto the surface of the water, until, in a scene deleted by the Studio after adverse audience reactions during preview screenings, the monster throws the girl into the water, in the same guiltless way he has tossed flowers onto the lake. The next scene opens on the child's father carrying her pathetic drowned body through the streets of the village. In what was to become a clichéd finale, the villagers, armed with pitchforks and staves, pursue Frankenstein and his Creature to the old mill where, after a pitched battle, the monster throws the hapless Frankenstein from a parapet, and then, presumably, perishes in the flames when the villagers set fire to the mill. This was the alternative ending: Universal had filmed two versions, one of which had Colin Clive perish, but, after preview, they decided to retain the happy ending.

Throughout the film, and in particular the scenes where the Creature first appears and tries pathetically to make contact with his Creator, and the scenes of terror as Fritz tortures him with flame, Karloff makes the role of the Monster uniquely his own. It was a role which was to make him a star for the rest of his movie career and to establish him as one of the all-time great horror film performers. With typical modesty, Karloff credited make-up expert Jack Pierce. "When you get right down to it," he said, "it was Jack Pierce who really created the

Frankenstein monster. I was merely the animation in the costume."

Like Christopher Lee after him, Karloff suffered considerably to bring the Monster to the screen. He had to get to the Studio every morning at 5.30 am and the make-up took over three and a half hours to apply. His height was increased by wearing heavy asphalt-spreader's boots and, to build up his body for the part, under his costume he had to wear a thick quilted suit.

Despite the success of *Dracula*, Universal had no idea of the box-office winner they had on their hands, nor any conception of the star power that Karloff was to generate. All that changed with the film's release: by the end of 1931, *Frankenstein* was one of the biggest money-spinners, and the horror/monster movie was firmly established as a unique genre.

There were many other factors, apart from Karloff's superb characterization, that ensured *Frankenstein's* success at the box-office. Despite the weakness of Colin Clive in the part of Henry Frankenstein, the film became and remains a classic. Photographed by Karl Freund and shot in studio sets, where the prevalent Germanic influence in Hollywood is very noticeable, the

movie is a superb creation to look at, with its twisted indoor perspectives and the bleak and sinister exteriors with their washed-out death-like tones and strangely formal appearance.

The reviewers knew a good movie and a superb performance when they saw it. *Frankenstein* earned from the New York *Daily News* the statement that ". . . *Frankenstein* . . . guarantees satisfaction after an hour's worth of gripping, intriguing horrors", while the *New York Times* said: "Beside it, *Dracula* is tame . . ."

As for Karloff, he said: "My dear old monster, I owe everything to him. He's my best friend!" The Creature was a "friend" that Karloff was to play twice more before handing his boots and bolts to other, less skilled, interpreters.

1932 saw Charles Laughton portray an evil scientist in *Island of Lost Souls*, a version of H. G. Wells's *The Island of Doctor Moreau*, so weird and unpleasant to the British Board of Film Censors that they banned the movie outright. The film was directed by Erle C. Kenton and has Laugton as a sadistic vivisector trying to impose his views on evolution by operating on animals in an attempt to turn them into humans. He succeeds only in creating terrible monstrosities–ranging from the

Head Hunting! Lon Chaney Junior looks for a potential brain donor as he abducts Janet Ann Gallow and fends off Bela Lugosi's Ygor in Ghost of Frankenstein *(Universal 1942)*

Panther Woman (Kathleen Burke), whom Laughton hopes to mate with the film's hero, Richard Arlen, an ape-man, a dog-man, and other unpleasant monsters. They are led in their chanting by Bela Lugosi, unrecognizable under face-covering black hair, and it is Lugosi who leads the final and terrifying attack, when all the creatures force Laughton into his own "House of Pain", the laboratory in which he had created his monsters, there to vivisect him. Eerily photographed by Karl Struss, *The Island of Lost Souls*, although repellent in many aspects, still rates as a masterpiece of the genre, in no small measure due to Laughton's bravura performance.

Karloff was back again as the Creature in *Bride of Frankenstein*, again with director James Whale. This time, and to the film's ultimate detriment, it was decided that Karloff's monster should have the power of speech, instead of the feral snarls in which it had indulged in *Frankenstein*. And, in a misguided attempt further to "humanize" his characterization, Karloff was also permitted, misguidedly, to smoke and drink wine, being taught by a blind hermit (O. P. Heggie), who also taught the monster to speak.

The reappearance of the Creature, presumed burned to death in the flaming mill in *Frankenstein*, is explained by showing that the monster had, in fact, fallen to the mill's cellar, which was conveniently flooded, there to rise again and terrorize the countryside until chased away from temporary refuge with the blind hermit. Then comes a meeting with gin-sipping Dr Praetorius, played with a cackling humour by Ernest Thesiger. Praetorius, who had already created human life in miniature with a series of mannikins kept in glass jars, forces Dr Frankenstein, Colin Clive again, to help him create a mate for the Creature.

The creation of the Bride, played by Elsa Lanchester in a hair-style reminiscent of Queen Nefertiti, is by far the best portion of the movie, helped by the extraordinary camera angles of cinematographer John Mescall and editor Ted Kent. The vivid musical score by Franz Waxman beautifully counterpoints the action, culminating in a clash of wedding bells as the Bride comes alive. The moment of triumph in this creation is short-lived for, on being led to her intended groom, Elsa Lanchester's Bride recoils in horror, cutting the air with an animal shriek. "We belong dead," intones Karloff, pulling a lever which, after allowing Dr Frankenstein and his bride Elizabeth (Valerie Hobson) to leave, destroys the laboratory in an explosion that was to become something of a trademark in the last reels of monster movies.

The story of *Bride of Frankenstein* was written by William Hurlbut and John L. Balderston, and the main narrative was framed in a flashback in which Mary Shelley (Elsa Lanchester) was persuaded by Lord Byron (Gavin Gordon) to tell what had happened after the Creature's supposed death in the burning mill. Originally, the film was to have ended on a downbeat, with Dr Frankenstein and his bride, perishing with the Creature and his Bride in the laboratory explosion, but the final version had the nick of time escape of Colin Clive and Valerie Hobson.

In 1938, Karloff was back, for the final time, as Mary Shelley's monster in *Son of Frankenstein*. *Son of Frankenstein* was originally scheduled to be shot in colour, the first Universal feature to receive this treatment, but, after filming had begun, it was found that Karloff's make-up did not work in colour and, along with scenes featuring Dwight Frye, who never appeared in the finished film, the colour sequences were abandoned and the movie was photographed in black and white by George Robinson.

This time Basil Rathbone, cold and incisive, plays the bearer of the Frankenstein name, returning to inherit his castle and to match wits against Lionel Atwill's Inspector Krogh. Krogh seeks the death of the monster who has torn his arm from his shoulder, leaving him with a wooden one in which, while playing with Wolf Frankenstein, he uncomfortably (for the audiences!) sticks his darts! Frankenstein brings the Creature from a coma with electrical energy, assisted by a hunchback, Ygor, who boasts of a crooked neck, the legacy of an unsuccessful attempt to hang him. Ygor, played by an unrecognizable Bela Lugosi in a fine and plaintive performance, is guardian to the monster. The Creature is in good form after revival, wearing an outsize sheepskin jerkin and, under Ygor's evil power, killing the jurors who have sentenced Ygor to death. He finally meets his nemesis after kidnapping Frankenstein's son Peter (Donnie Dunagan), wrenching Krogh's arm (fortunately, the wooden one!) once more from its socket, when Krogh pushes him into a convenient nearby pit of boiling sulphur!

The 1940s saw the flourishing of man-made monster movies, many of them second features. All kinds of scientists and doctors, mad and otherwise,

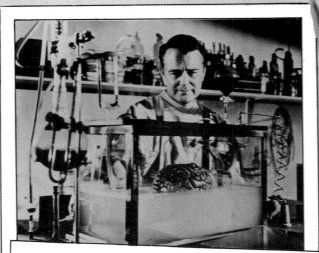

contributed new and more incredible monsters to the screen, thus keeping the genre bubbling. George Zucco maintained the man-into-ape tradition by placing executed killer Philip Terry's brain into an ape which then wreaked terrible havoc in *The Monster and The Girl* in 1940. The same year saw colour come to horror movies in Ernest B. Schoedsack's *Dr Cyclops* which had mad scientist Albert Dekker in thick pebble-lensed glasses in his Peruvian hideout, shrinking his enemies into doll-sized monsters! True to tradition, they caused his death when they effectively blinded him by destroying his glasses.

Universal brought their favourite monster back again in 1942, when Lon Chaney Jr donned the 18-pound boots and was brought to life again from his preservation in the pit of boiling sulphur in Erle C. Kenton's *The Ghost of Frankenstein*. The

74

reviving is done by Frankenstein's second son Ludwig (Sir Cedric Hardwicke) aided by Lionel Atwill's malevolent Dr Bohmer. This time the monster gets Ygor's brain by mistake, in place of the criminal brain in his skull, and proceeds to scare the living daylights out of Ludwig when it speaks with Ygor's voice! Chaney was no Karloff and, while he was able to convey the Creature's power and brutishness, he could not give any of Karloff's brand of pathos to his characterization.

Bela Lugosi turned himself into a monster when, as Dr Brewster in the 1942 film *The Ape Man*, he found himself becoming the title creature as a result of his experiments. He looked very much like his bewhiskered self from *Island of Lost Souls* and lost his life when a real gorilla attacked him at the end of the movie! Edward Dmytryk gave the female of the species a chance in 1943 when John

Carradine as a gland specialist transformed an orangutan into a beautiful woman (Aquanetta) in *Captive Wild Woman*. The film also featured Rondo Hatton whose features, distorted by acromegaly, made him the only horror film actor who could get by without make-up. Unfortunately, Mr Hatton was woeful as an actor, and, faced with dialogue, his performances were dire. Aquanetta reverted to simian form at the end of the movie but reappeared the following year with Milburn Stone and super-screamer Evelyn Ankers in *Jungle Woman*. This mini-series petered out with a last ape-woman-monster played by Vicky Lane in 1945's *Jungle Captive*.

At last, in 1943, Bela Lugosi played Frankenstein's Creature, 12 years after he had first turned it down. The film was the first of Universal's multi-monster movies, *Frankenstein Meets The Wolf Man*, with

Lon Chaney Jr repeating his role as the cursed lycanthrope, Lyle Talbot. It was too late for Lugosi to make much from the role of the monster, and the film was basically a reason for Universal to stage a battle royal between their two major monsters, Frankenstein's Creature and The Wolf Man. This time, the monsters perished by water as the marauding villagers breached a dam and flooded the laboratory in which the two were battling.

In addition to the Frankenstein cycle, the Forties and early Fifties produced a poor crop of horror creations as the plague of the B-feature took hold of the fantasy film. The ultimate in monstrous terror probably occurred in 1948's *Abbott and Costello Meet Frankenstein* when the monster, Glenn Strange, rises from his crate to come face to face with Lou Costello: a true connoisseur of horror, it is the Monster who backs away in fear!

The brain of a dead financier, kept alive by unscrupulous Lew Ayres who allows it to exert its malevolent thought control, made an unusual monster in the 1953 version of the Curt Siodmak story, *Donovan's Brain*. Filmed three times in all, its latest reincarnation was in the visually eerie *Vengeance* in 1962, with Peter Van Eyck as the scientist who keeps the evil brain alive in its murky tank and Anne Heywood as the put-upon heroine, under the expert direction of horror director Freddie Francis.

E. A. Dupont, director of the 1926 German silent classic *Variety*, made the 1953 movie *The Neanderthal Man* in which Robert Shayne not only makes a sabre-tooth tiger out of his laboratory cat as part of his proof that he can create a Neanderthal Man, but also follows the pattern by turning himself into the title monster! After preying on assorted animals, the Neanderthal Man turns to killing humans before falling victim to the sabre-tooth tiger!

It was in 1955 that Jack Arnold made *Tarantula*, one of the classic movies in the "make-a-monster" genre. Arnold set *Tarantula* in a small desert town, on the outskirts of which Leo G. Carroll's Professor Deemer experiments with artificial nutrients which he hopes will be the answer to larger food animals and an end to the world's food problems. As with so many of the screen's monster-makers, Carroll was to create his horrors because of unforeseen snags, and experimentation was entered into from the highest possible motives.

The film is filled with felicitous horrors: the appearance of the hideously misshapen figure of the dying experimenter behind the film's credit titles establishes the prevailing atmosphere of fear and tension, and, characteristically, Arnold never lets this slacken, culminating in the escape of the giant house-size tarantula from the laboratory and its depredations in the bleak desert surroundings. Universal's special effects are well up to standard, accentuating the almost universal dislike of spiders, and the destruction of the monster with napalm bombs is convincing.

England's Bray Studio, home of Hammer Films, was at first sight an improbable setting for the renaissance of the monster movie in particular, and horror films in general. However, encouraged by the international success of *The Quatermass Experiment* (in the U.S. known as *The Creeping Unknown*) in 1955, Hammer's Chairman, Sir James Carreras hit upon the idea of re-making the Universal "classic" horror films this time in colour. Hammer Films were to revive the horror genre and keep it going for nearly two decades, and their formula was a simple one: first rate actors, first rate directors, and budgets, which, while certainly not large by Hollywood standards, never betrayed that fact on the screen. The results could be gauged by Hammer Films' immense success at the box office and the fact that they created two world horror stars in Peter Cushing and Christopher Lee. Terence Fisher, who had started as a film editor in the 1930s and had graduated to direction with brilliant results, was justly raised to pantheon status as a director of horror and fantasy films.

The Curse of Frankenstein in 1956 starred Peter Cushing as the Baron and Christopher Lee as the Creature: for both actors, this was to mark their transition from small-part screen actors to major stars, although both had already established themselves firmly in their profession. Cushing was born in Surrey on May 26, 1913, and, as a boy, had started his acting career by presenting a puppet show to his family, with his brother, his share of the "take" being some three shillings! Finally, he achieved his ambition to become a professional actor when he joined the Connaught Repertory Company in Worthing.

Cushing eventually went to the U.S. and, finding no work on the New York stage, he made his way to Hollywood where, appropriately under the direction of James Whale, he had his first screen role in *The Man in The Iron Mask* which starred Louis Hayward. After other Hollywood movies, including *A Chump at Oxford* and *They Dare Not Love* with James Whale, Cushing returned to England, where, after appearing in Laurence Olivier's *Hamlet* in 1947, he became one of the busiest and best television actors in Britain. He appeared in a few British movies, including *The End of The Affair* and *Moulin Rouge.*

Because of his success as a television actor, movie companies tended to steer clear of Cushing, as they did with all actors who, they believed, had defected to the electronic screen. Hammer Films was the notable exception to this exceedingly short-sighted policy, and Cushing was cast as Baron Frankenstein in *The Curse of Frankenstein.*

Christopher Lee played the Creature. As Lee tells it: "My agent sent me to see Tony Hinds. He knew that they wanted a tall man, a big man, for obvious physical reasons, and to ensure that the dominance and power of the character would be communicated. They also needed somebody who could act without words, a very difficult thing to

achieve." He goes on: "I could only act with my body and one eye, since, as it happened, the other was blind, and under this mask were undertaker's wax and cotton wool, glue and plastic, and all sorts of unpleasant things!" Because Universal still retained the original copyright on the Monster make-up that Karloff had created with Jack Pierce, Hammer was forced to start from scratch and create its own Monster, not only breaking the copyright but also taking into consideration that the film would be in colour.

Make-up man Phil Leakey appreciated that the creature would be the product of "real" surgery, and the result was totally divorced from the dome-headed gray-featured monster of Boris Karloff. Lee appeared as a Creature of incredible strength, the face a welter of scars and applied tissue, made more horrifyingly real when part of the head was shot away in a shotgun blast. Lee, like Karloff, had to

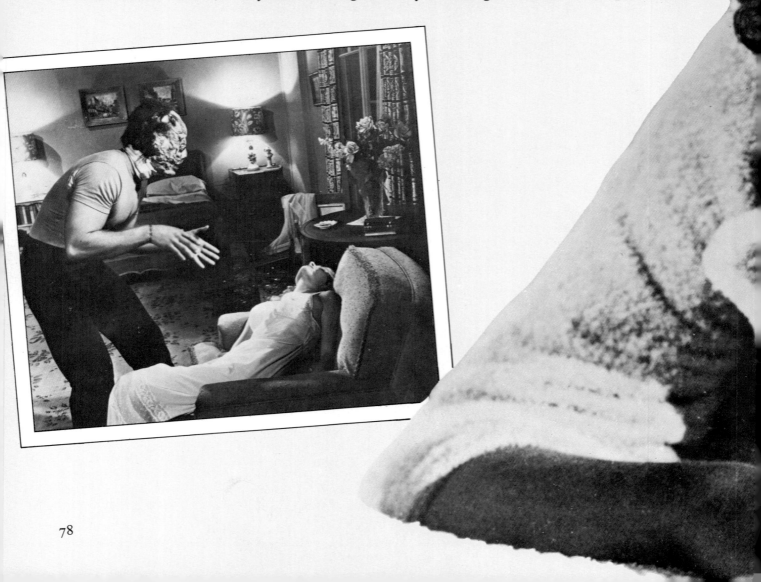

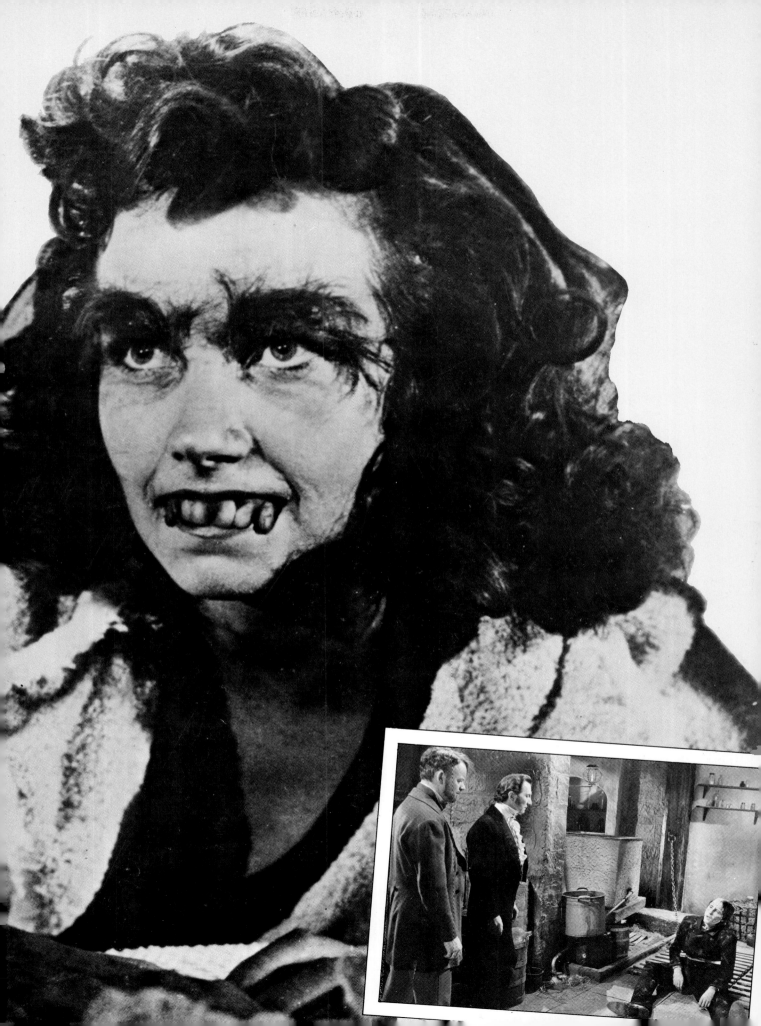

endure real discomfort in playing the part. ". . . I looked pretty unattractive. Some people say like a road accident . . . Phil Leakey and I did it together while we listened to the Olympic Games on the radio from Tokyo, at 4.30 in the morning, as I remember. It was very uncomfortable, and I wasn't able to wear the make-up for very long. I had to eat mashed potatoes and drink everything through a straw, because if I moved my face, everything came off!"

Fisher deliberately, as was his custom, avoided seeing the Universal *Frankenstein* films again before directing *The Curse of Frankenstein* and his approach paid off handsomely. *The Curse of Frankenstein* was a huge and deserved success, never betraying for a frame its low budget and very short shooting schedule. Jimmy Sangster had gone back to Mary Shelley for his screenplay, and not only ensured that Frankenstein regained his preeminence as the Creator, but also raised the Creature, back to its rightful place as one of the screen's great monsters. Cushing and Lee complemented each other superbly, the former totally convincing as the dedicated scientist willing to murder if it was necessary to achieve his object, the latter conveying both the brute strength and animal

Right. *Carole Grey meets an experimental disaster from the Delambre family in* The Curse of The Fly *(20th Century-Fox/Lippert 1965)*
Bottom right. Konga *(Merton Park/Herman Cohen 1960), the giant ape from Producer Herman Cohen's stable, breaks out*
Centre. *One of* The Alligator People *(20th Century-Fox 1959) proves that being thick-skinned isn't enough!*
Bottom left. *The matter transmission experiments carried out by Brett Halsey lead to* The Return of The Fly *(20th Century-Fox 1959)*

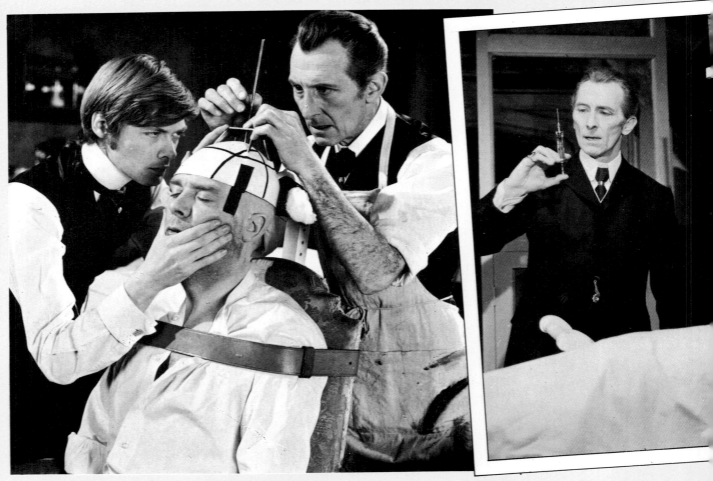

Left. *Simon Ward assists the definitive Baron, Peter Cushing, as he drills into the hapless Freddie Jones' skull in* Frankenstein Must Be Destroyed! *(Hammer 1969)*

instincts of the flawed creature, as well as its inherent pathos. Fisher used his Eastman Colour beautifully, effectively silencing those critics who still stayed in the monochrome Forties; and he never flinched in portraying the charnel house origins of the monster, abetted by Cushing's cool, unmelodramatic playing, whether fastidiously displaying a pair of severed hands, or surgically assembling the body of his creation. After *The Curse of Frankenstein*, monster movies were changed in two very significant ways. Firstly, Britain became, and was accepted as, the new home of the horror movie, with Hammer very much in the vanguard. Secondly, colour was to become almost an essential prerequisite for those movies which, for a new generation of moviegoers, were to feature Cushing, Lee, and Vincent Price, as well as Karloff, Rathbone and Lorre, as the technicolor horror stars.

Monster-making received a transfusion of new blood from Hammer. Producer Herman Cohen, with an eye firmly on the lucrative teenage movie market, cashed in on the Baron's re-emergence with *I Was a Teenage Frankenstein*, in which Whit Bissell, representing an American sprig of the clan Frankenstein, assembles his monster (Gary Conway) and turned in a profit of several hundreds of thousands of dollars for Mr. Cohen! That was in 1957, and in the following year, Kurt Neumann directed *The Fly*, a monster movie in CinemaScope and colour which outraged the critics, as horror movies tended to do, but delighted audiences all over the world. Velvet-voiced Vincent Price was on hand with Herbert Marshall to witness the unfortunate result of Al Hedison's experiments in matter transmission. The first try at projecting a live creature, the family pet, results in the total disappearance of the creature, leaving a "stream of cat atoms" and a disembodied mewing. His next attempt, on himself, results in a fly with one human arm and a human head, destined to be crushed to death with a stone by Price, in order to save it from impending consumption by the spider in whose web it has been caught. Hedison ends up with a grotesque fly's head and arm, the latter having a terrifying tendency towards a life of its own, like Kubrick's Doctor Strangelove. Rather than face the world in his grotesque state, Hedison has his wife, Patricia Owens, crush his arm and head to an unrecognizable pulp in a hydraulic press in a genuinely terrible and bloody climax.

Cushing was back again, in great form as Baron Frankenstein, saved from the guillotine at the end of

Centre. *Peter Cushing at work once more, in* Frankenstein Created Woman *(Hammer 1967)*. Right. *Robert Flemyng and Wanda Ventham survey the giant Death's Head Moth in Vernon Sewell's* The Blood Beast Terror *(Tigon 1967)*

The Curse of Frankenstein and back to monster-making in 1958's *Revenge of Frankenstein*. This time, the monster created by Cushing remains sane until its brain is damaged in a fight, and it turns into an eater of human flesh. The Creature is played by a rather handsome Michael Gwynn, and while he perishes, Jimmy Sangster's script allows Frankenstein to escape and set up practice in London's Harley Street as Doctor Frank. Bernard Robinson provided his usual high standard of set design, and once more Terence Fisher drove the film firmly along.

Howard Koch's *Frankenstein 1970* was remarkable mainly for Boris Karloff at last playing a Frankenstein, in this case Baron Victor von Frankenstein, scarred victim of Nazi torture and bent upon recreating his ancestor's legendary monster. This he does, in the bandaged form of Mike Lane, and to prove that the Frankenstein's genius can move with the times, the feat is accomplished with the aid of an atomic reactor. The most original touch in the movie was a glimpse of the photograph from which Karloff was modelling his Creature's features: it showed the younger Karloff's portrait. Despite his many years familiarity with monster-making, Karloff was no more suc-

cessful than his predecessors and perished with his Monster in a cloud of atomic steam.

1958 also saw the creation of an android monster, with a human brain implanted in an oversized robot, in Eugene Lourie's *The Colossus of New York*. The next year, with the very best intentions, George Macready distilled a special serum from alligator fluids, which he injected into accident victims so that, like the reptiles, they would grow new limbs. Instead, they turned into scaly semi-saurians, 1959's *The Alligator People!* 1959 also saw Susan Cabot turn herself into a lethal giant insect in Roger Corman's addition to horror films bestiary, *The Wasp Woman*, and Twentieth Century Fox, never a studio to keep a Fly down with a mere blow from a hydraulic press, made *Return of The Fly*. Vincent Price was around once more while, in black and white this time, Brett Halsey continued the saga of the Delambre family and turned himself into a monster like his father before him.

Michael Gough, a fine British horror movie actor with a nice line in gentle-until-roused maniacs, created 1961's *Konga*, a monstrous ape which grows to giant proportions, smashes a laboratory and proceeds to lay waste to great chunks of the London skyline.

1963 was one of Roger Corman's most prolific film-making years. In *The Haunted Palace*, an amalgam of Poe and Lovecraft stories, Vincent Price and Debra Paget find themselves menaced by hideous mutants in 18th-century New England, obscene monsters produced by Price's warlock ancestor as part of a plan to create a new master race. The movie chilled, aided by expert performances from Price, Lon Chaney Jr and Elisha Cook Jr, and evocative cinematography in Pathe Color from Floyd Crosby.

Ray Milland, experimenting with eye drops to increase his range of vision, turned himself into an all-seeing monster in *The Man With X-Ray Eyes*. At first delighted with his x-ray vision, (although, with permissiveness being what it was in 1963, audiences had to be content with shots that ended a few inches below the neck or above the knee), Milland is driven to insanity as his new eyes enable him to see far beyond the flesh. Finally, after his eyes have gone from gold to black, he takes the advice of itinerant preacher John Dierkes and, in a shocking finale, plucks them out to leave blank red pits.

In humorous vein, Corman had sorcerer Boris Karloff turn Peter Lorre first into a black bird with the unmistakable cigarette-rasped voice of Lorre, and then into a monster, half-bird and half-Lorre in *The Raven*. This was an affectionate and genuinely funny spoof of the genre, and Karloff, Price, Lorre and Hazel Court all entered whole-heartedly into the spirit of things. Only Jack Nicholson as the movie's juvenile lead looked wooden and bemused in the face of so much expertise and professionalism.

Peter Cushing was back for a third attempt in 1964 with *The Evil of Frankenstein*. Freddie Francis neatly directed producer Anthony Hinds' script, written as his alter ego, John Elder. Once more, Baron Frankenstein, perfectly played by Cushing, finds his Creature preserved in ice and brings it back to life. The twist this time is provided by the battle of wills between Frankenstein and mesmerist Zoltan (Peter Woodthorpe) for the control of the Creature whose dormant brain has been brought back to a semblance of life by Zoltan's hypnotic powers. A laboratory fire and explosion destroy the Creature after it has killed the Burgomaster and a constable and poisoned itself after drinking chloroform in mistake for brandy!

The Delambre family, creators of the Fly, came back in 1965 with *The Curse of the Fly*, still after their goal of matter transmission. The Fly never turns up in this movie, directed by Don Sharp: instead, there are decomposing radiation victims of transmissions, stables filled with monsters created the same way, while hero Martin Delambre (George Baker) has a nasty tendency to decompose at intervals. *Carry on Screaming*, 1966's entry in the successful screen series, featured a whiskery monster called Odbodd and his "successor", Odbodd Junior (Tom Clegg and Billy Cornelius), the pet creatures of Kenneth Williams' Dr Watt and Fenella Fielding's vampire-inspired Valeria. The movie attempted unsuccessfully to guy what it saw as horror movie clichés but finally died by its own hand.

Akim Tamiroff found himself turned into *The Vulture* in 1966 and the Golem came back twice. The first time was in a French television film *Le Golem* and the second in glorious Eastman Color in *It*. Allen Sellers was The Golem, discovered when a museum fire destroys a cache of museum exhibits. Roddy McDowall as museum assistant Arthur Pimm, a strange man who keeps his mummified mother comfortably in bed instead of in the grave, recognizes the statue as the 16th-century Golem, and reanimates it by putting a Hebrew scroll under its tongue. The Golem in this movie – written, produced and directed by Herbert J. Leger – is nothing if not modern in its uses. Apart from more traditional activities like murdering the new curator and abducting heroine Jill Haworth at McDowall's command, it also takes time off to destroy London's Hammersmith Bridge. Although it survives a small nuclear blast and is last seen heading out to sea, The Golem has yet to reappear!

A stranger monster was created by director John Frankenheimer in his 1966 movie *Seconds*, a terrifying and all too believable version of the search for eternal youth. Arthur Hamilton, a rich, middle-aged and jaded American chooses to change mind and body and reappear, surgically and mentally remodelled by Will Geer's sinister organization, a new young man with a new life. The initial stages of the movie are redolent with terror as Hamilton (John Randolph) makes contact with the organization and is changed into Rock Hudson; only the latter part of the movie, impeccably shot by veteran photographer James Wong Howe, goes off the rails in a welter of philosophizing and unconvincing orgies.

1967 was a busy year for movie monster-makers. Cushing's incisive performance carried *Frankenstein Created Woman*, the last of the Hammer series

to be made at Bray Studios. Terence Fisher's superb direction covered most of the inadequacies in Susan Denberg's portrayal of the beautiful but bisexual and malevolent Woman, who spends the movie revenging herself on those responsible for the guillotining of her innocent boyfriend whose soul now inhabits her body! Her end is unusual for a Frankenstein creation: John Elder's script has her commit suicide by throwing herself from a cliff into a torrential river.

Cushing turned up again, in a considerably lesser film, Vernon Sewell's *The Blood Beast Terror* in which mad scientist Professor Mallinger (Robert Flemyng) creates a giant moth as mate to his death-dealing, blood-drinking daughter, Wanda Ventham, who has a nasty habit of metamorphosing into a giant Death's Head moth. For once, Cushing is not monster-maker but Inspector Quennell of Scotland Yard.

Herbert J. Leger wrote, produced and directed *The Frozen Dead* at Britain's Merton Park Studios as a companion piece to *It* in which Dana Andrews took the mad scientist role of Dr Norberg, busily experimenting in his peaceful English country mansion with his supply of deep-frozen Nazi corpses. In order to assist with his experiments in reanimating the corpses, Andrews decapitates Elsa (Kathleen Breck) for her live brain: keeping her

Below. *Scott Anthony as Pleasence's assistant is far from a pretty face but infinitely preferable to the chlorophyll creature he later becomes!* The Mutations *(Getty Picture Corporation 1973)*

alive in the laboratory is his undoing! She exerts her mental control and activates a collection of severed human arms which strangle Norberg and his German master, General Lubeck!

In the Amicus Films omnibus version of Robert Bloch short stories *Torture Garden*, eerily directed with considerable visual flair by Freddie Francis, film starlet Carla Hayes (Beverly Adams) is made into a never-aging automaton and into a star by evil Dr Heim (Bernard Kay) after scratching the face of movie superstar Paul (Robert Hutton). The sight of the silver metal gleaming through the tears in his skin is genuinely disturbing, and the episode ends ironically with Carla Hayes attending a movie premiere and being greeted with shouts of "Isn't she a living doll!" by the excited crowds.

The screenplay for Hammer's 1969 *Frankenstein Must Be Destroyed* was written by Assistant Director Bert Batt. This time Peter Cushing, ably assisted

by Simon *Young Winston* Ward, was ahead of his time in medical science, successfully carrying out a brain transplant from George Pravda's Dr Brandt into the skull of Freddie Jones' Professor Richter. The movie displays Cushing and director Terence Fisher at their best, with a real Gothic feel for the genre, and the climactic battle between Creator and Creature in a blazing house provides an exciting end to the movie. *Frankenstein Must Be Destroyed* confirmed what had been obvious since *The Curse of Frankenstein*–whereas, in the Universal black and white movies, all the emphasis had been on the monsters, and the name of Frankenstein had become inextricably transposed onto the monster, Cushing and Hammer had made certain that it was the Baron who was the focal point in each movie and the connecting link between each film in the series.

Although the nominal stars of *Scream and Scream Again* in 1970 were Vincent Price, Christopher Lee and Peter Cushing, they took up comparatively little screen time in this tale of extraordinary monster-making by Price's urbane Dr Browning. The bulk of the movie is carried by Alfred Marks, in a disturbing toupee, as the Scotland Yard Superintendent investigating a gruesome series of London murders in which the victims are completely drained of blood. Director Gordon Hessler kept the film going at a pace which disguised the holes in the plot. There are effective moments of horror in Price's laboratory where he is busy creating his new race of supermen, and one brilliant shock effect when, having captured one of the supermen, the police handcuff him to the front bumper bar of an automobile. He escapes, leaving a severed hand still in the handcuff!

The return of Frankenstein in the following year, 1970, in Hammer's *The Horror of Frankenstein*, a jokey version written, produced and directed by Jimmy Sangster, sadly missed Peter Cushing's Baron. Instead there was a young Frankenstein, more interested in sex than in the pre-occupations of his family. Ralph Bates played Victor Frankenstein, building the Monster by numbers; Dave Prowse played the Monster with more bare torso than acting ability, and his disappearance, dissolved in a vat of acid, with just his giant boots bobbing to the surface, is perhaps the best scene in the movie.

1970 was much better served when Bruce Dern grafted the head of John Bloom onto the shoulders of Albert Cole to produce *The Incredible Two*

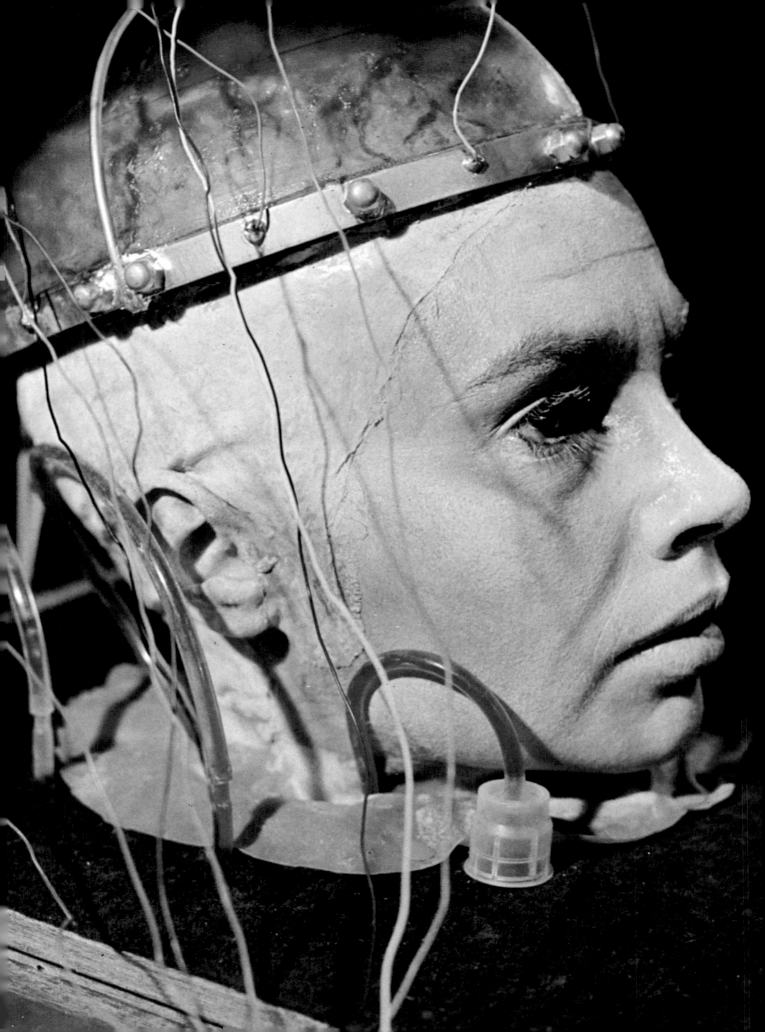

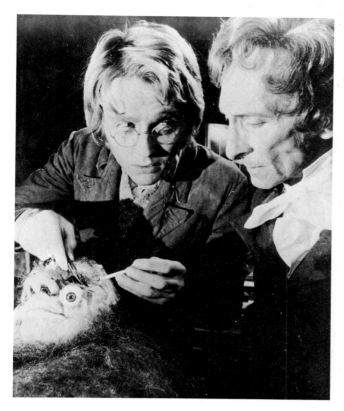

Headed Transplant in the best tradition of horror movies mad scientists. The monster was effectively convincing, created by Barry Noble, and former editor Anthony M. Lanza did so good a job with the movie that the idea was revived in the following year with Lee Frost directing Ray Milland and "Rosey" Grier as *The Thing With Two Heads*. The movie was played for humour, with Ray Milland as the Black-hating Mazwell Kirshner unwillingly finding himself sharing the same body with black convict Jack Moss, particularly as Kirschner finds himself unable to control Moss's body!

1973's *The Mutations* unpleasantly combined real circus freaks with a mad scientist story, in a disturbing amalgam of a conventional horror movie with strong echoes of Tod Browning's 1932 *Freaks*. Donald Pleasence played the monster-making Dr Nolter with melodramatic relish, creating The Lizard Woman of Tibet as a result of unsuccessful experimentation, and disposing of her in a circus side-show, and turning Scott Anthony into a human carnivorous vegetable, a giant Venus Fly-trap who gets his revenge by ingesting the luckless Mr Pleasence. Julie Ege decorated the movie in various states of undress, and *The Mutations* was directed by Jack Cardiff, a cinematographer who had worked with notable effect on many colour films.

1973 happily saw the return of Terence Fisher to the great tradition of Gothic colour horror movies which, by and large, he had created. He was reunited with the greatest Baron Frankenstein, Peter Cushing, and scriptwriter John Elder for

Frankenstein and The Monster From Hell. Dave Prowse again played the monster, this time a hulking, half-ape, half-humanoid Creature, fashioned under Cushing's direction in the insane asylum where he was working, by Frankenstein's assistant Dr Simon Helder (Shane Briant). Frankenstein plans to mate his monster with a mute inmate of the asylum, "The Angel" (Madeleine Smith), but although "The Angel" tries to save him, the monster perishes, torn savagely to pieces by the inmates of the asylum. The film is full of classic horror scenes: Cushing's first entrance, silencing the howling madmen with a mere movement of his arm, the underground laboratory with its bubbling vials and intestinal glass tubes, the monster itself, a splendidly gruesome arrangement, and an incongruously disturbing scene with the monster holding an incredibly fragile-looking violin.

How monster movies should not be made was demonstrated by director Jack Smight in the 1973 film *Frankenstein: The True Story*, the latest would-be "major" entry into the genre. All the auguries were good: the production company was Universal Pictures; the script was written by Christopher Isherwood and Don Bachardy and returned to Mary Shelley's novel; and the cast looked like a *Who's Who?* of great British performers – James Mason, Sir Ralph Richardson, Sir John Gielgud and Margaret Leighton, with Michael Sarrazin as The Creature, Leonard Whiting as Victor Frankenstein and David McCallum as Henry Clerval. Neither in the four-hour version of

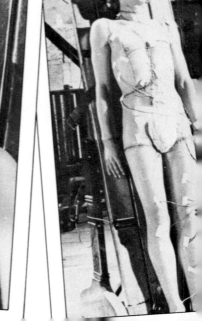

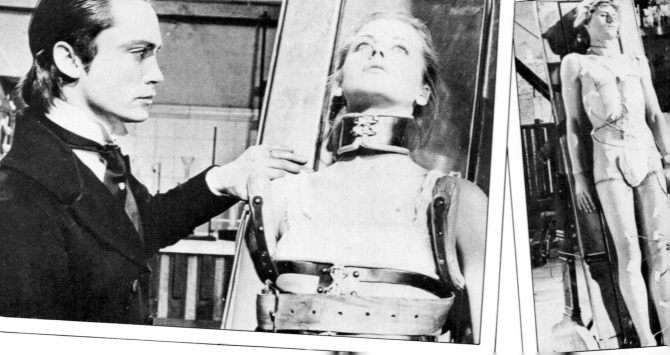

Pity the Baron! Scenes from Flesh For Frankenstein *(C. C. Champion and I (Rome)/Jean Yanne–Jean Pierre Rassan (Paris) – An Andy Warhol Presentation)*, *Andy Warhol's grisly and unatmospheric retelling of the Frankenstein story in 3-D, with Udo Kier as the Baron and Arno Juerging as his assistant Otto.*

the movie shown on American television nor the two-hour version released theatrically in Britain did all this talent combine to produce a great, or even more than adequate, Frankenstein film.

It is hard to see exactly what went wrong. Certainly the script, as published and interpreted, was not good. The concept of the beautiful Creature, disintegrating in the manner of Dorian Gray, never really came off, despite Michael Sarrazin's spirited attempts to give it life, and, sadly, Jane Seymour as the female Creature, Prima, gave a curiously negative performance. The best parts are the making of the monster in a ruined mill by Frankenstein and Henry Clerval, and the life-giving process, through solar energy, was a Technicolor rival to the machinery produced by Universal for the 1931 *Frankenstein*. Cinematographer Arthur Ibbetson, production designer Wilfrid Shingleton and special effects devisor Roy Whybrow made all the laboratory scenes the most memorable in the film. And Smight produced one scene of genuine power, kept from being risible by good direction and acting, when Michael Sarrazin's Creature bursts into the ball being held to launch Prima in society, and tears her head from her shoulders. The contrast between the horror of the act, the Creature with its decaying features and the ballroom filled with elegantly dressed dancers and onlookers, was well observed and the scene stands out in a movie which basically lets the genre suffer from neglect and leaves the viewer uninvolved.

Surprisingly, the monster-making genre was revitalized in 1974, with the best humorous horror movie since Roger Corman's *The Raven*, 11 years previously. The film was *Young Frankenstein*, conceived and co-written by Gene Wilder and directed, for the most part impeccably, as an homage to the Universal Pictures monochrome movies of the Thirties and Forties. Wilder played Victor Frankenstein's grandson Frederick, so embarrassed as a modern doctor by the family name that he always insists upon the pronunciation "Frahnkensteen". Left his grandfather's castle in Transylvania, Frederick travels back, to be met at the station by Marty Feldman as a hunchback with a moveable hunch, Igor, one-time assistant to the great Baron. After being led around the castle by the strange nocturnal wailings of a violin, Frederick discovers his grandfather's laboratory and full instructions on how to make a monster, carefully secreted to await his arrival by Frau Blücher (Cloris Leachman).

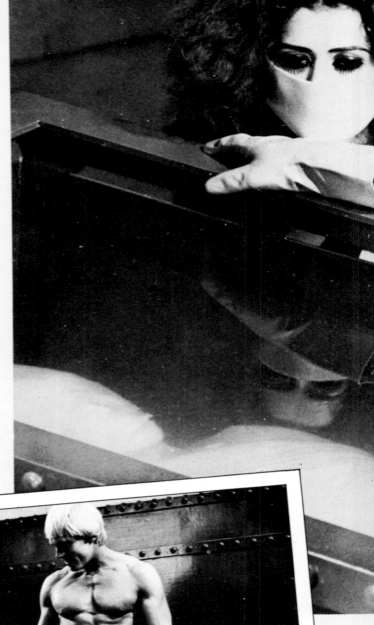

Right. *Frank N. Furter (Tim Curry) and Magenta (Patricia Quinn) wait together as* The Thing in The Tank *takes on human form in* The Rocky Horror Picture Show *(20th Century-Fox 1975)*. Below. *Furter with Peter Hinwood as his Creation Rocky in the horror-science fiction spoof* The Rocky Horror Picture Show *(20th Century-Fox 1975)*

The laboratory was a splendid replica, by Kenneth Strickfaden, of the set made for Colin Clive and Dwight Frye to give life to Boris Karloff in the 1931 *Frankenstein*. Frederick makes his Creature, complete with a damaged brain procured for him by Igor at the local Brain Depository, in a brilliant scene of creation that poked affectionate fun at the genre while never losing sight of the basic premise behind the movie. Then, with the damaged monster (Peter Boyle), spreading fear around the village, one-armed Inspector Kemp (Kenneth Mars), in a hilarious take-off of the scene between Lionel Atwill and Basil Rathbone in *Son of Frankenstein*, confronts Frederick in the library. Electrically shocked by mistake, the Creature rushes from the castle, there to meet Gene Hackman, impenetrably disguised behind a large beard. The scene between him and the Creature as he attempts to be hospitable towards his visitor is both accurate parody and achingly funny. Bereft of sight, Hackman pours boiling soup into Boyle's lap, smashes his glass of wine against Boyle's, and finally sets fire to him while trying to light his cigar, driving the starving and anguished monster screaming out of the hut into the night and the scene into classic comedy and horror.

Brook's touch is sure again as the Creature plays with a little girl (Anne Beesley), tossing flowers down into a well, only to turn the scene onto its head by having the monster catapult the child safely through a window and into bed as he attempts to play on a seesaw with her. The public unveiling of his triumph is staged by Frederick at the usual convention of scientific scoffers: after demonstrating that the monster could obey in a series of childish exercises, the lights go down, the monster's white smock is whipped off and, the lights up again, Wilder and Boyle demonstrate their ability in white tie and tails and *Puttin' On the Ritz!* The movie is superb, with the brilliant pastiche cinematography in black and white by Gerald Hirschfield and John Morris' music adding to the overall effect.

To show that movie monster-making can encompass anything the screen can make "real", and will continue to do so, 1975 brought a movie version of the stage success, with most of the original cast, in *The Rocky Horror Picture Show*, a bizarre horror movie, complete with Tim Curry as the transvestite Frank N. Furter, a monster, Transylvanians, a ruined castle that takes off into space, a stranded honeymoon couple and enough references to other movies to make it a rich mine for cineastes for a long time. If the genre can survive *The Rocky Horror Picture Show*, then clearly the years to come will see a steady stream of sane and mad scientists and other accidental creators producing as rich a menagerie of Creatures as have appalled the cinema since Méliès discovered the first secret of special effects.

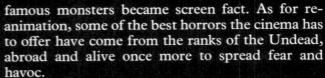

Transformation is one of the most basic ingredients in the cinema of terror. With stop motion photography, superimpositions and dissolves, as well as other, more recondite special effects, Lon Chaney Jr sprouted hair and became the Wolf Man, the Invisible Man peeled off his bandages and vanished from the screen, Dr Jekyll became Mr Hyde and many other less famous monsters became screen fact. As for re-animation, some of the best horrors the cinema has to offer have come from the ranks of the Undead, abroad and alive once more to spread fear and havoc.

As far back as 1889, the mysteries of ancient Egypt proved an irresistible lure to film-makers. Méliès made *Cleopatra*, retitled for Britain and the U.S. as *Robbing Cleopatra's Tomb*, in which a mummy is chopped into pieces and then resurrected by fire into a living woman! This apparent piece of movie magic presented no problems to a man trained as a stage magician, for whom the camera was merely another tool of illusion.

Movie reanimation had begun: transformation soon followed, with the first of many film versions of Robert Louis Stevenson's *Dr Jekyll and Mr Hyde*. This was a 15-minute film performed by a stock theatre company. The first two decades of the cinema showed the popularity of the story of the schizophrenic doctor. James Cruze took the part in the 1912 *Dr Jekyll and Mr Hyde*, becoming hairy and fanged as the potion did its work, and then murdering his prospective father-in-law—and then leaving the movie by taking poison in his laboratory as the police battered at the door! In 1913 Carl Laemmle formed Universal Pictures by amalgamating several small motion picture companies, notably his own "Imp" Company, Bison 101, Powers and Nestor, and put King Baggot into a version of *Dr Jekyll and Mr Hyde*. It was a good augurie for the studio that was to become the leading horror movie studio by the 1930s. Baggot impressed the critics in his transformation scene, aided in no small amount by camera tricks. 1913 also saw Universal entering the realm of the man-beast with *The Werewolf*, in which a Navajo squaw dissolves into a real wolf to avenge her lover's death.

Egypt was back in movies in 1918, and in Ernst Lubitsch's *Die Augen Der Mumie Ma (The Eyes of The Mummy)* Emil Jannings had a go at Pola Negri's heroine. 1919 saw the Undead raised to murderous life as Conrad Veidt's "Somnambulist" was brought to life from its home in *Das Kabinett Des Dr Caligari (The Cabinet of Dr Caligari)*. This expressionist horror movie, with its painted sets and contorted streets and houses, and uneasily forced perspectives, is one of the landmarks in the genre. The story of the murdering zombie and its depredations was perhaps the one single most influential horror movie until the Hammer colour

& THE BEAST

Boris Karloff adds another classic role to his portfolio as
The Mummy, *directed in 1932 for Universal by Karl Freund.
In Jack Pierce's make-up, Karloff appears here as the sinister
Ardet Bey with heroine Zita Johann*
Inset. Schizoid Star. *Fredric March changes from Man to
Monster in his Academy Award-winning performance as
Dr Jekyll and Mr Hyde* (Paramount 1932)

Invisible appearance. Vincent Price comes back under wraps for the title role in The Invisible Man Returns *(Universal 1940), here with Nan Gray*

revival in 1956. Even today the film still chills as Veidt, in black leotard and cavernous eyes, glides through the streets and over the twisted rooftops. If the painted sets were to achieve fame, it was not something that the designers Hermann Warm and Walter Röhrig could completely have anticipated: they were as much a product of money saving – canvas and painted shadows – in post-war Berlin, as a deliberate attempt to change the genre and create a totally new style. Nevertheless, the production design, photography and Robert Wiene's direction of Veidt, Werner Krauss as Dr Caligari and Lil Dagover as the much put-upon heroine, all gelled into a thrilling whole.

F. W. Murnau filmed his version of Robert Louis Stevenson's novella under the title of *Der Januskopf*. Imprudently, he did not bother to clear the copyright with the Stevenson estate and all copies of the movie were recalled and destroyed. The same year, 1920, Paramount filmed *Dr Jekyll and Mr Hyde* with the Great Profile, John Barrymore. He was already nearing 40 when he made the movie, but looked years older, and audiences thrilled to his transformation from matinee idol

Jekyll to hideous Hyde. After drinking the potion, Barrymore grabbed his throat, went into convulsions and marred the Great Profile by literally dislocating his features and suddenly and hideously, without special effects, becoming the brutish Mr Hyde. Only when the camera focussed on his hands did camera tricks take over – slow dissolves changed his hands into elongated talons. The script took in much more than Stevenson's original, borrowing some of Oscar Wilde's epigrams for the sub-titles and not a little from *The Picture of Dorian Gray*, especially in the character of Brandon Hurst's Sir George Carew. The film had two female stars in Nita Naldi and Martha Mansfield, but it was Barrymore's movie, whether exhibiting his considerable charm as the studious Jekyll or bestial and ugly as Hyde, haunting Soho music halls and Limehouse opium dens. Only in his death as Hyde, when he drank poison, did Barrymore allow himself to slump in death to reveal, for the last time in the movie, his famous profile.

In 1932, horror movies achieved their only Academy Award for acting when Fredric March got an Oscar for Paramount's *Dr Jekyll and Mr*

Un-hirsute lycanthrope Henry Hull is locked in the laboratory as the Werewolf of London *(Universal 1935)*

Hyde. The movie was conceived by the Studio as a prestige production, but was also intended to cash in on the sudden box-office popularity of the genre, brought about by movies such as *Dracula* and *Frankenstein.* The director, Rouben Mamoulian, worked with the writers, Samuel Hoffenstein and Percy Heath, and had to battle with Paramount Head, B. P. Schulberg, to be allowed to use Fredric March as Jekyll/Hyde. Even though March was then known mainly as a light actor and comedian, Mamoulian insisted that not only was he the perfect Jekyll but he could also play the brutish Hyde. He was justified in his expectations and March turned in a superb performance, aided by some stunning visual effects as he changed from Jekyll to Hyde.

Particularly effective, as well, was the opening sequence which used a subjective camera so that the audience were Jekyll as he made himself ready to go out, took hat and gloves and only revealed himself when the camera showed him in a mirror. When it came to the transformation, however, Mamoulian and March excelled themselves. In what appeared to be (and was) a continuous take, March's face metamorphosed smoothly from his

matinee idol appearance into the evil Hyde. By excluding stop motion photography, dissolves or superimpositions, Mamoulian achieved a totally believable transformation. The total Hyde make-up was placed on March's face from the beginning, but cosmetics were used which were only revealed when various graduated colour filters were held in front of the camera. By careful manipulations of these filters, layer after layer of make-up became visible in sequence and March was changed from beauty to bestiality in a single take.

March's performance, as both Jekyll, good looking, mild but driven by powerful internal compulsions to separate his good and evil selves, and the brutish, perverse Hyde, deserved its award, and this version ranks easily as the best of all films of *Dr Jekyll and Mr Hyde.*

Karloff added another monster to his portfolio in Universal's *The Mummy* in 1932. This had a screenplay by John L. Balderston and was brilliantly directed by Karl Freund in his first directorial assignment. Karloff plays Im-Ho-Tep, buried alive in ancient Egypt after stealing the sacred Scroll of Thoth in order to bring his love to life again.

Bramwell Fletcher plays the archaeologist who opens the tomb some 3,000 years later, reads aloud the words from the Scroll of Thoth and brings the Mummy back to life. As the Mummy, shown only as a trail of dust and rotting bandages, takes his "little walk", Bramwell Fletcher becomes insane at the sight.

Ten years later, with his face incredibly wrinkled and deathlike, in very effective make-up by Jack Pierce, Karloff returns, this time disguised as Egyptian archaeologist Ardet Bey, now in modern Cairo and leading another British expedition to his tomb so that they can bring out the mummified body of his love. After her mummy has been taken to the Cairo Museum, Ardet Bey tries to bring her back to life again. Failing this, he pursues her reincarnation, Helen Grosvenor (Zita Johann). Despite the precautions taken by Dr. Muller (Edward Van Sloan), who has discovered that Ardet Bey is in reality Im-Ho-Tep, Helen Grosvenor faces Ardet Bey in the museum, where he intends to kill her so that they can spend eternity together. As she prays in desperation to Isis, the statue comes to life and destroys Im-Ho-Tep, leaving a happy last reel reunion between Helen and her lover played by David Manners. Karloff was superb, particularly as the Mummy, with all the power of a robot under the rotting bandages that covered his body, but with his eyes still alive and showing the depth of his love. The scenes of Ancient Egypt are impressive as Karloff shows them to Zita Johann in a flashback reflected in a misty pool.

The following year saw Karloff back in his native England, and making *The Ghoul*, the first British movie to try and get on to the horror movie bandwagon. Gaumont-British took no chances with their investment. Not only did they have Karloff for insurance but also the familiar theme of Ancient Egypt and Karloff's return from the dead to avenge the theft of the jewel, "The Eternal Light".

In Hollywood, 1933 marked the first time a star emerged from a movie through the use of his voice alone. *The Invisible Man* had been turned down by Boris Karloff since he would appear only in the film's closing scene. Instead, James Whale directed fellow Englishman Claude Rains, whose voice carried all the necessary menace and madness of the character of Dr Griffin, user of the drug monocaine to render himself invisible and thus pave the way to world domination. Like all such induced transformations, the drug not only made Dr Griffin invisible, but drove him on to insanity and megalomania, with murder, robbery and the derailing of a train all part of his scheme of things! Whale's quirky sense of humour, which had worked against the success of *Bride of Frankenstein*, was more suited to the story and style of *The Invisible Man*, and the movie is effective, both as a chiller

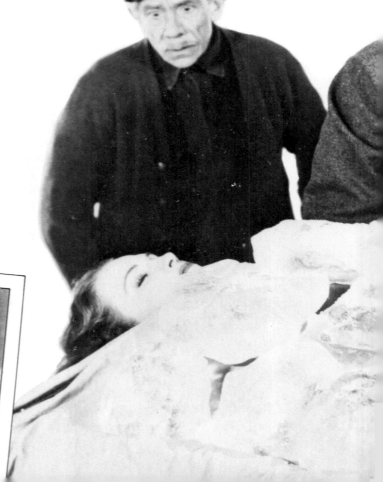

and as the first screen appearance of a new movie monster. But John P. Fulton's special effects were what the audiences marvelled at: double exposure, matte shots, masked negatives and model shots as well as far more complicated techniques were all deployed. None was more successful than at the end of the movie when Griffin, at last betraying his presence by his footprints in the snow, is shot. As he dies, he appears, first the bones, then arteries, veins and nerves and, finally, the dead features of the scientist.

Universal were back in the Werewolf business once more when, in 1935, Henry Hull became *The Werewolf of London.* Despite good special effects as Hull changed into the beast, this movie, which had as its core a variation on the "Jekyll and Hyde" story, was not successful, either in establishing the Werewolf as a "classic" movie monster, or in making Henry Hull a new horror star, as the studio had hoped might happen. The direction by Stuart Walker was perfunctory, and Hull's make-up was nowhere near as good as that which Jack Pierce

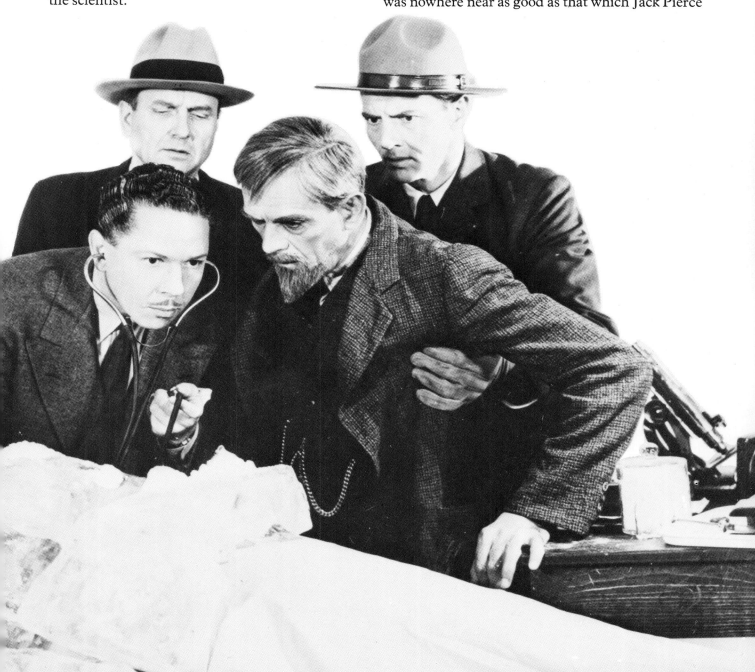

Above. *Spencer Tracy stars in Victor Fleming's* Dr Jekyll and Mr Hyde *(MGM 1941), one of Tracy's few critical and box-office failures.* Right. *The Victim reacts traditionally at the sight of fur-featured Lon Chaney Junior,* The Wolf Man *(Universal 1941), in this posed publicity still*

was later to create for Lon Chaney Jr. This was not Pierce's fault, however, because Hull refused to spend the necessary hours in make-up, leaving Pierce no option but to devise a relatively un-hairy face for the Werewolf.

Karloff was reanimated after execution in the electric chair by Edmund Gwenn's Dr Beaumont in Michael Curtiz's 1936 movie *The Walking Dead*. After frightening the men who had ensured his wrongful conviction so that they died in terror, Karloff returns to the dead, but not before he warns Dr Beaumont to leave the dead to their own devices! In Britain, Robert Stevenson (later to direct *Mary Poppins!*) made *The Man Who Lived Again*, in 1936. This had Karloff in the role of the mad scientist Dr Laurience, busy bringing people to life by transposing minds from body to body! And, in 1939, Karloff was Dr Savaard in *The Man They Could Not Hang*, creating a mechanical heart to bring life to the dead. Taking no chances, however, he creates his own corpse to test his machine! The unfeeling authorities try the luckless doctor for murder and execute him, but, fortunately, his assistant Lang (Byron Foulger) soon has him alive again with the aid of the mechanical heart. Spending the rest of the movie eliminating the jurors who have sentenced him to the gallows, Karloff then destroys his machine and returns to the grave.

Karloff was back in 1940 for Columbia, this time transforming himself into a younger man with a serum made from the blood of a convicted murderer, in *Before I Hang* directed by Nick Grinde. In the same year, Universal made *The Invisible Man*

Returns in which Vincent Price used John P. Fulton's special effects to escape from jail and trap the real murderer, in this case his own cousin, portrayed by Sir Cedric Hardwicke. The Mummy, too, was brought back to life by Universal, with Tom Tyler stepping into the bandages that had been Karloff's. The former cowboy star was chosen because of his resemblance to Karloff as he had looked in the 1932 film, *The Mummy*, so that shots from this could be matched into *The Mummy's Hand* by director Christy Cabanne. This time he was Prince Kharis, brought to life by George Zucco with his magic brew of nine tana leaves, only to return to the dead once more when a boiling vat of tana juice was spilled over him by hero Dick Foran. 1940 was a busy year for Karloff and Nick Grinde, who directed *The Man With Nine Lives* in which Karloff was Dr Kravaal, experimenting to find a cure for cancer, but instead finding that his drug put people into suspended animation under ice until such time as they needed to be defrosted and brought to life again. This time, he was shot at the end of the movie!

John P. Fulton brought his invisible special effects into play again in 1940, when doctor John Barrymore turned Virginia Bruce into *The Invisible Woman*, a humorous version of the theme of invisibility which had her marrying John Howard and producing an invisible child!

Bela Lugosi had played Murder Legendre in the 1932 movie *White Zombie* for B Feature producers, the Halperin Brothers, and it was they who revived this sub-genre in 1936 when Dean Jagger saw a

Left. *Lon Chaney Junior carries off Elyse Knox in* The Mummy's Tomb *(Universal 1941)*. Bottom left. *Nina Foch is the screen's most attractive werelady in* Cry of The Werewolf *(Columbia 1944)*. Bottom centre. *Bud Abbott and Lou Costello with a brave Boris Karloff in* Abbott And Costello Meet Dr Jekyll And Mr Hyde *(Universal 1953)*. Right. *Back from the Dead, Alvaro Guillot is the product of* Pharoah's Curse *(Bel-Air 1956)*

way to provide himself with cheap militia in *Revolt of The Zombies*. Monogram saw that sufficient time had elapsed since the Zombie had shuffled his way through a horror movie, and so they had Jean Yarbrough direct Henry Victor raising the dead once more in 1951's *King of The Zombies*. Mr Victor, naturally, had only the best motives in his creation of the Walking Dead – he had hoped to use them as troops in World War Two!

Lon Chaney Jr stepped into the pantheon of screen monsters when he took the role of Lawrence Talbot, *The Wolf Man*. Universal decided that it was time to have another stab at the Werewolf, after their 1935 failure with *Werewolf of London*, and this time they struck gold. Although the werewolf had existed in literature since well before the birth of Christ, and all over the world, Curt Siodmak's screenplay for *The Wolf Man* invented a whole new lore for the lycanthrope. Where Henry Hull had turned into the Beast after a bite from a weird creature while he searched for the mysterious

flower, Marifas Lupina in Tibet, Chaney was bitten by a real wolf, even if it was a transformed Bela Lugosi! Where Hull had died from "normal" bullets fired from police guns, the new Universal Wolf Man would only die from a silver bullet, or, failing that, from a blow with a silver-headed cane.

After Lugosi bit him, Chaney begins to itch and soon, yielding to an irresistible urge, he tears off his clothes. With the inspired help of John P. Fulton, Jack Pierce, and cameraman Joseph Valentine, and over 20 hours removing previously applied make-up with acetone to effect the transformation, he becomes the Wolf Man, more animal than Henry Hull could ever have dreamed possible. He is soon rampaging in fine form, tearing the throat from a gravedigger, sending Evelyn Ankers into one of her best screaming fits, and only dying when his father (Claude Rains) smashes him on the head with his silver-topped cane. The transformations were impeccable, and despite six-hour sessions in the make-up chair under the ministrations of Jack Pierce, who patiently glued on individual yak hairs, pieces of kelp and claws, Chaney loved his creation, saying: "He was my baby!"

In 1942, Chaney abandoned his yak hairs for the bandages of Kharis in *The Mummy's Tomb*, in which not only did the director, Harold Young, have to match up Boris Karloff and Tom Tyler for flashbacks from their stabs at the role, but in addition had to take into account the fact that

Chaney would not be under wraps for the whole of the movie, as stunt man Edwin Parker took over for the more strenuous action! This time Kharis is reanimated in America by Turhan Bey, and this time, after unsuccessfully pursuing the reincarnation of beauty, Elyse Knox, Kharis is destroyed when vengeful villagers set fire to a house, taking the Mummy to its doom in the flames.

1942 confirmed the slide in Bela Lugosi's career. In *Bowery at Midnight*, a shaky, alcoholic doctor revives corpses of criminals at a Bowery eatery—but he was not played by Lugosi, who instead had the double role of Professor Brenner and the provider of the corpses, Kurt Wagner, the proprietor of the eatery. Lugosi finally dies at the hands of his revived victim.

Val Lewton's low budget unit at RKO had been the training ground for many directors who would later go on to much bigger things at other studios. Robert *The Sound of Music* Wise, Jacques *Night of The Demon* Tourneur and Mark *Earthquake* Robson were among Lewton's "graduates", and it was Tourneur who brought the next zombie movie to the screen in 1943's *I Walked With a Zombie*. Frances Dee played a nurse, retained by West Indian plantation owner Tom Conway to look after his sick wife. Believed to be a Zombie by the superstitious islanders, the wife takes a nocturnal walk through the cane fields with her nurse, in a scene as terrifying as any in horror movies, made all the more so by effective use of natural, if accentuated, sounds of the wind whistling and swishing through the sugar cane, and the persistent throbbing of the native drums.

Lon Chaney Jr was back in his yak hairs as Lawrence Talbot, unwilling Wolf Man, in 1943's *Frankenstein Meets The Wolf Man*, but Universal merely used the movie as an excuse to stage a fight to the finish between the Wolf Man and Frankenstein's Creature; the monster was originally to have been played by Chaney as well, but Universal had decided against such complication and expense, and so it was Chaney versus Lugosi, with Chaney's Wolf Man drowning after the climactic battle.

1944 saw *The Invisible Man's Revenge* where Jon Hall went on a murder and mayhem spree under the influence of the drug discovered by John Carradine. Lugosi was back among the zombies again for Monogram's 1944 opus, *The Voodoo Man*, keeping his wife alive after she had died some 22 years previously! Lugosi imbued the film with a rare intensity and power which helped it over some

of the inherent silliness in the plot as he and his assistant Nicholas (George Zucco) kidnapped girls and tried to infuse their souls into the living corpse of the dead wife. Finally, he resorted to voodoo, accompanied by John Carradine, this time on the drums! *Cry of The Werewolf* brought Nina Foch to the screen as werewolf lady, Celeste La Tour, inheriting the taint of lycanthropy from her mother. No six-hour sessions with sticky yak hairs and kelp for Miss Foch—conveniently, and cheaply, she became a real wolf off-screen.

In 1945's *House of Dracula*, again directed by Erle C. Kenton, Onslow Stevens actually ensured a happy ending for the unfortunate lycanthrope. Correctly diagnosing that Chaney turned into the Wolf Man at the full moon because his cranial cavity was too small and pressed against his brain, Stevens cures him of his affliction by enlarging his skull. So, for once, Lawrence Talbot lives happily ever after—at least, for this movie!

1951 had Abbott and Costello back again, killing off the Invisible Man as a genre in *Abbott and Costello Meet The Invisible Man*. The Invisible Man was Arthur Franz, and the star of the picture was John P. Fulton, whose special effects included Lou Costello fighting for his life (he won, unfortunately), aided by the Invisible Franz, and Costello becoming invisible at the end of the picture. He didn't vanish for long, however, returning with Bud in 1953 in *Abbott and Costello Meet Dr Jekyll and Mr Hyde*. The double doctor was played, with considerable bravery, by Boris Karloff, terrorizing London while hunted by Abbott and Costello, policemen studying London police methods while on secondment from America at the turn of the century. *Abbott and Costello Meet The Mummy* administered the kiss of death to the genre, as far as Universal were concerned, with Eddie Parker under the bandages for the grisly ceremony.

Zombies were created by that obsession of the 1950's horror movie, atomic power, in Edward L. Cahn's 1955 *Creature With The Atom Brain*. And Walter Rilla's scientist ruler of Gudavia, Dr Boronski, created his brand of Zombies using gamma rays on local children in *The Gamma People* (1956). That film showed some feeling for tradition, however; director John Gilling had the villagers march, *Frankenstein*-style, to his schloss and set it on fire, and Boronski died in his blazing laboratory.

Steven Ritch was *The Werewolf* in 1956, shot down by Don Megowan after considerably being allowed to say goodbye to his family, and Boris

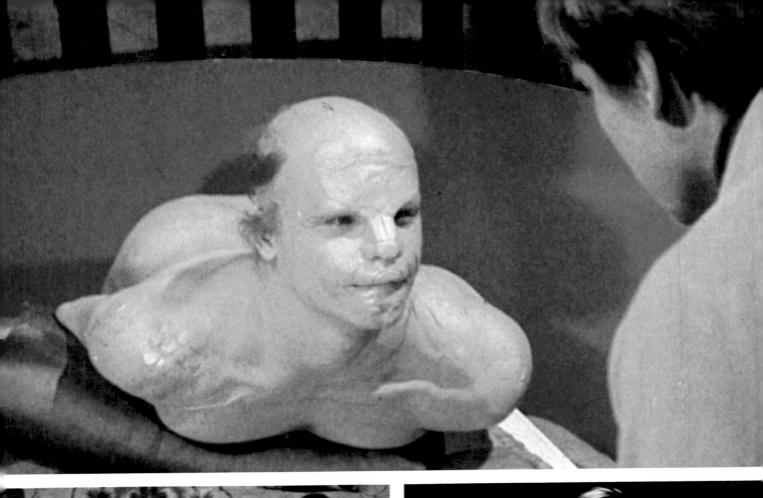
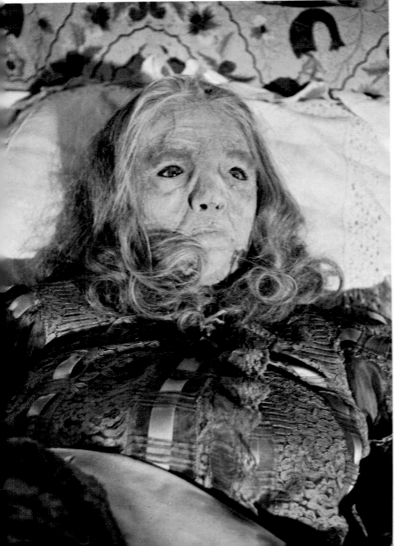

Karloff fended off the Undead and carnivorous plants on *Voodoo Island*, filmed on Kauai in the Hawaiian Islands. In *Zombies of Mora-Tau*, the living dead were used to stand guard over a diamond mine, a far cry from the days when they went into battle against the hordes of Nazi oppression.

After a break of two years, the genre was revitalized, in colour, by Terence Fisher's *The Mummy*. Jimmy Sangster wrote the script, basing it upon John L. Balderston's 1932 screenplay for Karloff's *The Mummy*, and Bernard Robinson designed some notable sets, both for the Ancient Egypt of Christopher Lee's Kharis and the Victorian England of Peter Cushing's John Banning. Yvonne Furneaux played the dual role of the Princess Ananka, for whom Kharis had his tongue cut out and was mummified alive, and her reincarnated self, Isobel, carried off at the instigation of the Mummy's modern day master, Mehemet

(George Pastell). Fisher's taut direction, the acting of Lee who, playing the Mummy for the only time in his career, conveyed totally both the power of the automaton-like monster, and the Mummy's inherent pathos, and Cushing as his antagonist, all ensured that *The Mummy* would become another Hammer "classic". The climax was particularly well-handled, with Cushing fighting desperately and unavailingly against the monster, blowing great holes in its body with a shot-gun, only to have it still come at him. Even after he has plunged a spear through the Mummy, Cushing is only saved by the appearance of Yvonne Furneaux. Remembering his centuries' old love, the Mummy leaves the attack and carries the girl off, to leave her safely while he sinks to his new death in the depths of a swamp. Once more, Lee suffered to create a classic monster. He says: "In *The Mummy*, I did have a double, for one shot—that business of going under

Below. *Carnivorous plants claim a victim on* Voodoo Island *(Bel-Air 1957)*

the swamp at the end. But otherwise it was me and, my God, I could not move when that mask was on. I could not hear properly. I could not talk."

Hammer entered the lists with their own version of the Jekyll and Hyde story, 1960's *The Two Faces of Dr Jekyll*. Despite careful direction from Terence Fisher, and impeccable recreations of Victorian London from the ever-dependable Bernard Robinson, the film was a qualified failure. What went wrong was that Wolf Mankowitz, the script-writer, tried to be too clever in his screenplay, and his gimmick of making Hyde the clean-shaven and sexually magnetic womanizer, while Jekyll was the morose and bearded scientist, never gelled. Paul Massie did the best he could with his part, and he was ably supported by Christopher Lee, but Hammer were to leave the subject alone until 11 years later.

In a small part in *The Two Faces of Dr Jekyll*, executive producer Michael Carreras had noticed a young man whom he thought might have star quality. The young man was Oliver Reed and the role that took him to stardom was that of Leon in Terence Fisher's *The Curse of The Werewolf*. John Elder produced a superb screenplay which was an adaptation of Guy Endore's novel *The Werewolf of Paris*. Richard Wordsworth beautifully captured the brutality and inner agony of the beggar who rapes the gaoler's daughter, a deaf-mute who gives birth to the werewolf Leon. The child soon shows the horror of the lycanthrope, returning to his home with blood on his mouth and terror in his mind,

leaving dead and mutilated sheep as witness to his nocturnal depredations. Fisher filled the film with deft touches of horror – the font boiling over as the baby Leon is christened, the climactic chase of the adult werewolf across the roofs, to be killed, compassionately, by his adoptive father (Clifford Evans) with the traditional silver bullet. Oliver Reed gave a finely observed performance, bringing animal strength and appetites to his metamorphosed werewolf self, and tender pathos to the interlude of his love affair with Christina (Catherine Feller), an interlude which brings a temporary respite to his transformation into a wolfman at the full moon. Reed was able, too, to show the agony of a man knowing himself to be tainted and yet totally unable to prevent that taint from taking possession of himself.

Zombies were brought back by the Italians in 1963, when John Drew Barrymore raised an army of the Undead to wage war on the Romans in *Roma Contro Roma (War of The Zombies)*, one of the many variations on the basic sword-and-sandal movie tried in the Sixties. By way of a complete contrast, Jerry Lewis wittily sent up the Jekyll and Hyde story in 1963's *The Nutty Professor*, which he directed. The scenes of transformation were particularly good, and the monsters that intervened before he became the final monster, crooner Buddy Love, were excellent.

1964 saw Michael Carreras as director of the next Hammer Mummy picture, *The Curse of The Mummy's Tomb* with a screenplay by Carreras in his

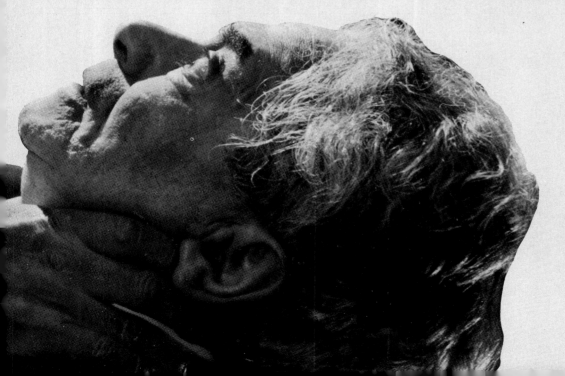

alter ego Henry Younger. This time Dickie Owen, who had doubled for Lee in *The Mummy*, took the role of the Mummy. Terence Morgan appeared to be the hero Adam Beauchamp but after the Mummy has been reanimated, and has killed Fred Clark, Jack Gwillim and George Pastell, Beauchamp reveals himself to be none other than the 3000-year-old brother of the Mummy, Ba, cursed for murder in Ancient Egypt to an eternal life! Despite this, he looked considerably better-preserved than his mummified brother, who finally despatches him in the sewers before bringing the roof down about their heads! Despite lovely camerawork from Otto Heller, the film never rose to the heights of Fisher's *The Mummy*.

Freddie Francis explored the subject of lycanthropy in 1964 in one episode of the multi-storied film *Dr Terror's House of Horrors*. In the episode *Werewolf*, written by producer Milton Subotsky, Jim Dawson (Neil McCallum) returned to his ancestral home in the Scottish highlands to meet the buyer of the house, attractive widow Deirdre Biddulph (Ursula Howells). He finds out, too late, that Miss Howells is, like her ancestor, a vengeful werewolf and falls victim to her attack. The story

was neat, the sets eerie and effective, and Francis directed the tale for all it was worth.

In 1964 in *Il Castello Dei Morti Vivi (The Castle of The Living Dead)*, Christopher Lee is the 19th-century Count Drago, busy filling his castle with corpses which he has carefully preserved. He joins his mummified collection when he is cut by a scalpel dipped in his own mummifying fluid. Donald Sutherland was on hand in a bit part as the Sergeant, and, in its own small way, the movie provides some horrific entertainment.

Peter Byan's scenario provided director John Gilling with the material he needed to make a minor masterpiece for Hammer, *Plague of The Zombies* in 1966. The setting was a sinister Cornwall, lushly photographed by Arthur Grant, with Andre Morell and Brook Williams fighting zombie-master John Carson to save Diane Clare. For Jacqueline Pearce, later to transform herself

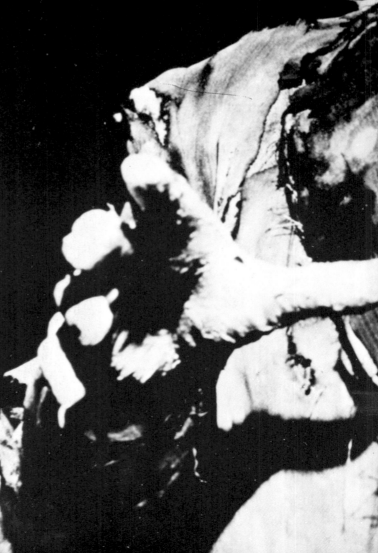

Below. *Dickie Owen takes over from Christopher Lee as The Mummy for Michael Carreras'* The Curse of The Mummy's Tomb *(Hammer-Swallow 1964)*

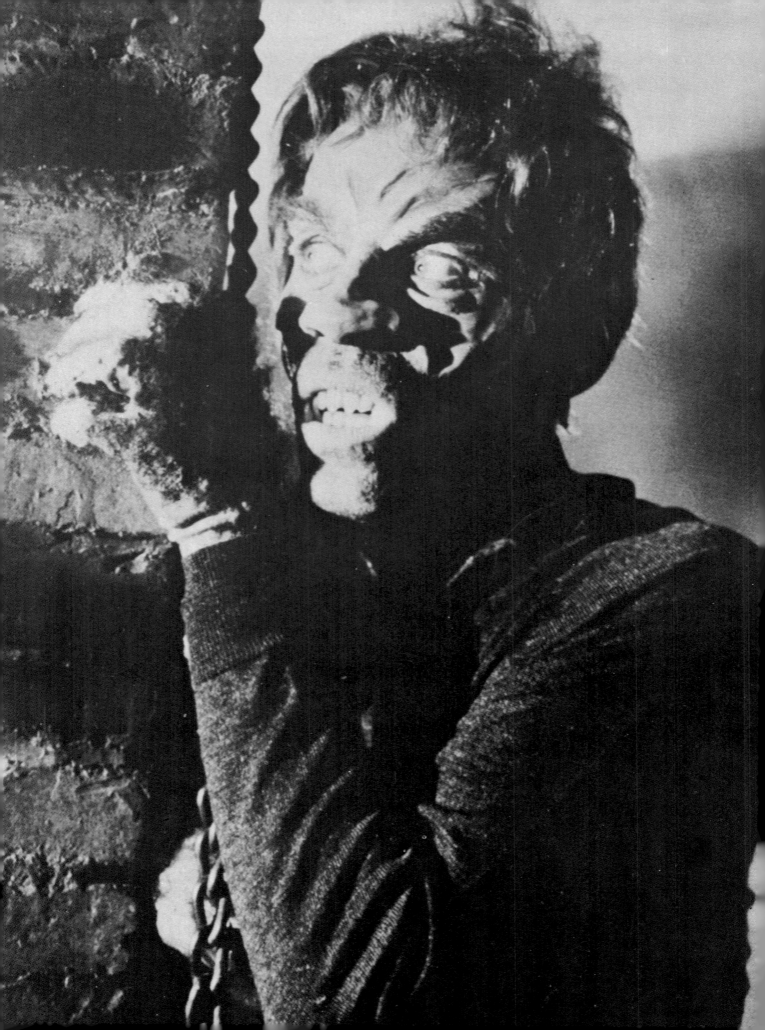

Opposite. *Curt Lowens is the* Werewolf In a Girl's Dormitory *(Royal 1961), a movie also known as* I Married a Werewolf *and the more prosaic* Lycanthropus. Below left. *In John Gilling's* Plague of The Zombies *(Hammer 1967), the graves yield their Dead in an eerily chilling dream sequence.* Below right. *Christopher Lee is menaced by Michael Gough's severed hand in an episode of Freddie Francis'* Dr Terror's House of Horrors *(Amicus 1964).* Bottom. *Trapped by Terence Fisher's* The Gorgon *(Hammer 1964), Richard Pasco shields himself from Barbara Shelley's petrifying gaze*

into the terrifying *The Reptile*, the outcome was
not so happy: she was beheaded, to save her from
remaining one of the Undead! John Carson
relished the role of the villain, raising the dead
to life again with strange voodoo ritual, and the
climax, with the tin mine on fire and the staring
Zombies staggering blindly through the flames, is
powerfully effective.

John Gilling had a go with the Undead of Ancient
Egypt for Hammer in 1967, writing the scenario for
The Mummy's Shroud from an original story by
John Elder. Roger Delgado as Hasmid Ali brings
the Mummy Prem back to life to stand once more
as guard to his young master, Kah-to-Bey, taken
from his defiled tomb by British archaeologists.
The Mummy embarks on its usual ritual of killing,
only to meet death itself, crumbling away to dust
in sinister special effects by Les Bowie when Maggie
Kimberley utters the sacred words of death.

The momentum was running out of the genre
again, and 1969 brought only a minor film, *Night
of The Living Dead*, enlivened, if a story of zombie
attack could be said to be enlivened, by the direction
of George A. Romero. He managed to stretch the
obviously low budget and endow the movie with
a cumulative terror as the zombies gather around
the house where the humans have taken refuge.

Hammer returned in 1971 with their last
variation, at the time of writing, on the theme of the

Below. *Peter Cushing and friend in another multi-episode Amicus movie, 1973's* From Beyond The Grave
Right. *David Rintoul, in make-up by Roy Ashton, is the Werewolf in Freddie Francis'* Legend of The Werewolf *(Tyburn 1975) (Photograph courtesy Tyburn Film Productions)*

Mummy, with *Blood From The Mummy's Tomb*, begun by Seth Holt and completed after his death by Michael Carreras. Valerie Leon is effective both as the supernaturally endowed Ancient Egyptian Queen Tera, buried alive with the hand that bore the ruby ring which gave her her power cautiously severed, and as the 20th-century Margaret, daughter of the discoverer of the tomb. The movie carries a high charge of power as Tera takes over the body of Margaret to avenge the desecration of her tomb. And the final shot, with Margaret now a living Mummy, swathed in bandages after a catastrophe which destroyed the house in which Corbeck

(James Villiers) had tried to revive the unaged body of Tera with the Scroll of Life, provides a suitably horrific finale to the movie.

1971 also saw Hammer have another, unsuccessful attempt to make something more of *Dr Jekyll and Mr Hyde* than Robert Louis Stevenson had intended when Roy Ward Baker directed Brian Clemens' scenario of *Dr Jekyll and Sister Hyde*. The movie, with its inexpensive solution to the special effects needed to transform Jekyll into Hyde (Ralph Bates as Jekyll transposing neatly into Martine Beswick's Sister Hyde), is not helped by Clemens' perverse humour and insistence upon

Left. *Lee and Cushing grapple in* I, Monster *(Amicus 1970)*
Below. *Peter Cushing chisels away at* The Creeping Flesh
(Tigon British/World Film Services 1972)

getting everything possible into the plot. Jekyll, in his search for the elixir of life conveniently employs the well-known bodysnatchers, Burke and Hare, to procure the corpses of women that he needs for his experiments, and, for good measure, Jack the Ripper overtones are thrown in as Jekyll is forced to murder prostitutes to get fresh material!

Cushing was on view again in 1972's *Tales From The Crypt* for which he won a richly deserved George Méliès Award for his portrayal of Arthur Grimsdyke. Freddie Francis directed the movie, and in the episode *Poetic Justice*, written by Milton Subotsky and adapted from the comic magazine by Al Feldstein, Johnny Craig and William Gaines, Cushing finds himself being hounded to his grave by neighbour James Elliott (Robin Phillips) who resents what he sees as Cushing's lowering of the tone of the locality by his ragged clothes and constant crowds of children round his house. Finally he drives Cushing to suicide, but Cushing rises again from the grave to extract full revenge on Phillips. Cushing's performance was beautifully judged, sure in every detail and almost unbearably touching.

In Don Sharp's *Psychomania* in 1972, the motor-cycle gang The Living Dead are exactly what they say they are, having returned from the dead thanks to a pact made with the Devil. Their depredations and scaring leaps from the grave, motorcycle and

all, are brought to an end when the leader's mother (Beryl Reid), horrified to see what has happened, revokes her pact with the Devil as her son (Nicky Henson) is about to strangle her. She ends up as a toad, while the gang is turned to stone!

Amicus gave ex-editor Kevin Connor his first directing assignment in 1973's *From Beyond The Grave*, another compilation of short films with Peter Cushing as an urbane and sinister link-man, playing the proprietor of the antique shop, "Customers of Temptation Limited". In the episode, *The Door*, Ian Ogilvy as William Seaton buys a carved door and, having fitted it into his room, finds that it opens into an elegant Restoration drawing room. In it he finds that Sir Michael Sinclair (Jack Watson) had used his occult powers to trap victims and ensure his continued defeat of death. Only after Ogilvy has destroyed the door with an axe, leaving the room to disintegrate

around a writhing and horribly mutilated dying Sir Michael, are Ogilvy and his wife Rosemary (Lesley-Anne Down) safe from the power of the room beyond the grave.

Universal entered the field of transformation again in 1973 when Scott Sealey played *The Boy Who Cried Werewolf*. When he tells the sherriff of his encounter with a werewolf that turned into a man again when it fell over an embankment and impaled itself on a wooden post, the boy is not

Above and left. *They'll have you in stitches! Two scenes from* The Living Dead at The Manchester Morgue *(Star Films (Madrid) Flaminia Produzioni (Rome) 1974)*

believed and finally finds himself in consultation with a psychiatrist! Returning to the scene of the impalation, Richie now finds himself faced with another werewolf, this time his father, Robert (Kerwin Mathews). Once more he is disbelieved, and a final trip to the mountains leads to his father turning into a werewolf yet again, rampaging through the town, immune to bullets, only to die when he is impaled on a broken crucifix belonging to yet another sign of modern times, a Jesus Freak!

Voodoo Girl had Don Pedro Colley as Baron Samedi raising some scary mud-caked zombies from the earth, the animated corpses of Guinea slaves, still in their chains, brought back to life from the 17th century. The movie is full of horrific moments, including the murder of Charles Robinson by female zombies in a massage parlour, and once more American International showed that there was still plenty of life in the genre. The Spanish/Italian co-production *Fin de Semana Para Los Muertos (The Living Dead at The Manchester Morgue)* was made the following year, in 1974, and is filled with gruesome images, not least of which is a cemetery crowded with the rising Undead, and a hospital filled with the zombies, now on a cannibalistic spree! Shot on location in Britain, director Jorge Grau directed the movie for all it was worth.

The genre seems to be getting back into its stride, and no doubt transformations and returns from the dead will continue to populate the horror film with more choice monsters.

Kirk Douglas takes on the roles of Dr Jekyll and Mr Hyde *in a musical version of the story made in 1973 (Timex/NBCTV)*

123

MONSTROUS C

The theme of Beauty and the Beast runs deep through horror movies, and although not always an impulse towards monstrosity, the love of animate and inanimate objects has motivated many a screen monster, from The Beast from 20,000 Fathoms to several Hunchbacks of Notre Dame.

Victor Hugo's *The Hunchback of Notre Dame*, published as *Notre Dame de Paris* in 1831, is one of the most filmed stories of monstrous love. There was a French version in 1906, entitled *Esmeralda* after the object of Quasimodo's piteous passion, and there were subsequent versions made in America and Britain, but it was not until Lon Chaney Sr put his stroke of genius on the role that the Hunchback became a classic movie monster.

Chaney had been born on April 1, 1883, the fourth son of deaf and dumb parents, and it was from his closeness to his mother that young Alonso became one of the most proficient actors in mime ever to come to the screen. By the time he came to make *The Hunchback of Notre Dame* in 1923, he had appeared in some 128 silent movies.

When Universal Pictures under the legendary Irving Thalberg decided to make a 12-reel movie of *The Hunchback of Notre Dame*, they knew that only Chaney could play the role and so struck a two-movie deal with him. The production was epic—the enormous sets that covered 6,000 square feet of the Universal lot were meticulously researched and created by E. E. Sheeley, Sydney Ullman and Stephen Gooson, and included a detailed recreation of the cathedral of Notre Dame, surrounded by eight blocks of streets and houses.

Lionel Atwill as the mad sculptor with potential victim Fay Wray in the Michael Curtiz Technicolor chiller Mystery of The Wax Museum *(WB 1933). Inset left. Broody Monster, Olga Baclanova ends up at a circus side-show, carved up into a 'Human Chicken' by the* Freaks *(MGM 1932). Inset right. Lon Chaney Senior,* The Hunchback of Notre Dame, *carries off Patsy Ruth Miller as his beloved Esmeralda in the 1923 silent Universal movie*

HANGES

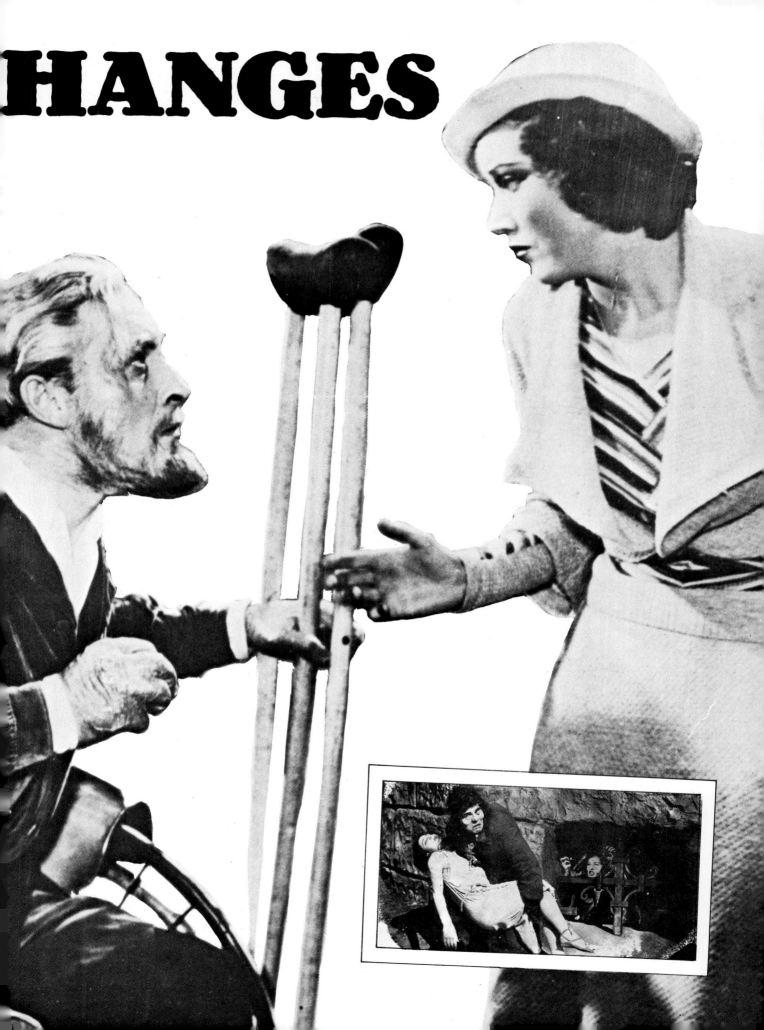

As always, Chaney created his own make-up, suffering a three and a half hour session before he could go before the cameras. He contorted his body into a metal breastplate and leather harness that added a further 30 pounds to the 40 pounds that the hump, made of rubber and covering his back and shoulders, already weighed.

Chaney's performance as Quasimodo, horrifying to look at and yet pathetically vulnerable in his love for Esmeralda, won him world-wide renown and made his the definitive movie version of the story. Despite the hideousness of his appearance, he was never merely a monster—his portrayal showed the hunchback always as a real and suffering human being, trapped with his emotions in an ugly shell of a body.

In 1925, Chaney created his second great movie monster as the disfigured Erik in the title role of Universal's *The Phantom of The Opera*. This had been adapted by Elliott J. Clawson from Gaston Leroux's novel, and it became one of the finest and best recalled of all silent movies. Chaney raised the basically melodramatic tale of the deformed composer, living under the Paris Opera House and filled with love for the young soprano, Christine Daae (Mary Philbin), for whom he kills in order to ensure her success as an opera star, to the level of a classic movie. Both his performance, which once again was a masterly sustained piece of mime, and his make-up, which he created himself, are superb.

The set was closed during much of the filming, the reason given by Universal being that Chaney's make-up was far too horrific to be seen. (They neglected to point out that it would certainly be seen when the picture was released!) In fact, there were directorial problems during the making of the film, with Rupert Julian, the original director, being replaced by Edward Sedgwick after he and the star had fallen out. While overall, lags in the narrative drive of the movie might reflect some of this trouble, the big moments still instil horror: the final chase through the sewers and streets of Paris, pursued by the sort of vengeful mob that would soon become a commonplace in Universal horror movies; the strangely disturbing scene where the two lovers meet, unaware that the Phantom, his billowing cloak hand-painted in red to add impact to the scene, hovered above them like an Angel of Death; Chaney's appearance as Death in a masked ball, his face a grinning bare skull, again accentuated by the whole sequence being tinted in red. But the greatest of all shocks comes as Mary Philbin tears away his mask to reveal the Phantom's true face. The scene still retains its power, as the Phantom tells her: "You shall stay here to brighten my toad's existence with your love."

To produce the living skull that lay behind his mask, Chaney inflicted much pain on himself. A wire device drew his mouth into the death-like grin while false teeth rimmed it like jagged stumps. His eyes were forced open by wires, his nose artificially spread out with a spreader of his own design, which also painfully moved the tip of his nose upwards. His cheekbones were highlighted with celluloid discs placed inside his mouth. And yet, despite the hideous discomfort this make-up must have caused him, once more Chaney was able to show the man beneath the monster.

Five years later, Chaney was dead, killed by a bronchial cancer that had robbed him of his ambition—to become in talking pictures "The Man of a Thousand Voices" just as, in silents, he had been "The Man With a Thousand Faces".

Fay Wray exercised her lungs and made sure of her title of horror films' most accomplished screamer twice in 1933. Both times she was the unfortunate love object of a totally unsuitable suitor, in the first case the terribly-scarred, masked Lionel Atwill, and in the second, a giant ape.

In Warner's *The Mystery of The Wax Museum*, directed at a cracking pace by Michael Curtiz and photographed in an early two process Technicolor by Ray Rennahan, heroine Fay Wray is amorously pursued by Lionel Atwill in his best villainous form as the fire-disfigured sculptor-owner of the Wax Museum, busily shaping wax models using corpses stolen from local morgues. The film's climax is an unmasking scene nearly the equal of Mary Philbin's tearing off of Lon Chaney's mask in *The Phantom of The Opera*. Miss Wray screams mightily as she batters helplessly against Atwill's smooth features, only to have their symmetry shatter into waxen fragments, to reveal his hideous real face, scarred and mutilated. Studio publicity had it that Miss Wray was so appalled by the make-up that she fainted when she saw it on the first take—fortunately she had recovered sufficiently to rouse her rescuers with her cries.

But undoubtedly Miss Wray's (or anyone else's, for that matter) greatest suitor was 1933's *King Kong*. Created by the genius of model animation, Willis O'Brien, the giant ape's statistics read like a nightmare: 50 feet in height, his chest measurement was 60 feet (unexpanded!); his face was seven feet high, from chin to hair line, his arms 23 feet in length, while his legs were relatively puny, being only 15 feet long! Even his features were gigantic, with a six-foot long mouth, two-foot nose and 10-inch eyes.

Willis O'Brien had been working with animated models since 1914, when Edison released his five-minute long movie *The Dinosaur and The Missing Link*. By 1925, O'Brien had graduated from clay models to models made of rubber over articulated wooden frames, and made a successful version of Sir Arthur Conan Doyle's *The Lost World*. He then went on to prepare and build the models for his next project, to be called *Creation*. The movie was never completed, but some of the situations and models were used by O'Brien in *King Kong*.

Merian Cooper, who co-produced and co-directed *King Kong* with Ernest B. Schoedsack, had become interested in gorillas when he was filming documentary movies in Africa, and he planned to make a movie with a live gorilla battering its way through New York. But in 1931, when he

joined RKO Studios he found O'Brien there with his *Creation* models. These so impressed him that he realized that he could dispense entirely with his live gorilla and instead use O'Brien's special effects. The Studio's shareholders were delighted with the results of a test film O'Brien made, and the film was given the go-ahead.

The story is the ultimate fairy tale, an impossible love story of Beauty and the Beast. From the time Fay Wray is first spied by King Kong, as she waits, a human sacrifice to the giant ape, god of the natives of Skull Island, she is subjected to his amorous advances, even giving Censors some heartache when, in a brilliant montage of model shots and live action, King Kong decorously begins to peel off Miss Wray's clothes! In fact, the making of the sequence could not have been less erotic: Miss Wray was filmed separately, her clothes being pulled off by wires, carefully lit so as not to appear in the shot. Then a waist-high model of the trees, plants and rocks was placed in front of a back projection screen and one of the

articulated models of King Kong was animated painstakingly so that its movements finally corresponded with the movements of the clothes, as they were torn off.

Model animation was not the only cinema trick employed by O'Brien in making the movie. To bring the story of the giant ape convincingly to the screen in his natural island home and his time in New York, culminating in the famous climb up the Empire State Building, a screaming Miss Wray in his giant hand, O'Brien, assisted by Marcel Delgado, produced a number of models of Kong, a 20-foot high bust of his head and shoulders in whose open mouth a man could hide, a giant mechanical hand so that Fay Wray could be shown in his grasp, and be pulled from her skyscraper apartment, and also used mattes, glass shots, optically achieved special effects, some brilliant process photography and rear projection. Such was the movie's impact, however, that most of its audiences only began to try and figure out how it was done after they had seen the movie. Max Steiner's pounding score, particularly as it built up to Kong's first stunning appearance on Skull Island, and the competent acting of Miss Wray, Robert Armstrong and Bruce Cabot all complemented O'Brien's triumph.

Such was the financial and critical success of *King Kong* that Cooper and Schoedsack spun into

production with a dismal failure of a sequel, *Son of Kong*. The pathetic progeny was discovered by Robert Armstrong when he returned to Skull Island, but the Son was no chip off the old Kong. Instead, he was a mere 20 feet high, with all the feral instincts of a gambolling lamb, and the script by Ruth Rose is best forgotten.

In 1939, RKO essayed a remake of *The Hunchback of Notre Dame*. Charles Laughton, in a papier-mâché hump and make-up by Wally Westmore, played the Chaney part, and while he never rose to the heights that Chaney had reached, his acting and that of Maureen O'Hara as Esmeralda and Thomas Mitchell as the King of The Beggars was excellent. William Dieterle directed it with immense power and a brooding concern for the grimness and squalor of the period, complemented by some of the most magnificent sets in movies, created by RKO's Van Nest Polglase, who had been responsible for the Astaire-Rogers musicals from the studio.

Val Lewton's RKO unit came up with an eerie story of perverse love in *The Cat People*, a movie that managed to cram in considerable terror without ever resorting to monsters, building its effect on careful editing and pacing, and a brilliant use of cinematography and sound effects. The 1942 movie which began Val Lewton's five year reign as King of the B-Features at RKO, was photographed by Nicholas Musuraca and edited by Mark *The Prize* Robson. Jacques Tourneur directed the tale of Balkan-born Simone Simon, whose impassive face made her ideal for the role, and her love for Kent Smith, and the passions roused in her by that love which turned her into a ravening panther. Most memorable are the scenes where the great cat is implied by light, shadow and sound, stalking a victim among the flickering light around an indoor swimming pool, or softly following a girl through New York's Central Park, until the sudden hiss of air from a bus frightens the girl—and the viewers—more than would seem possible without a direct and monstrous confrontation.

1943 saw Universal back in the sewers of Paris to make a colour version of *The Phantom of The Opera*. This time, having become a horror star with *The Invisible Man* 10 years before, Claude Rains donned the mask and played the organ in the catacombs, teaching a terrified Susanna Foster to sing, and finally being hunted down by Nelson Eddy, whose presence completely threw the movie off balance.

Below. *In* Revenge of The Creature, *Jack Arnold's brain-child solves the parking problem in truly monstrous manner in the 1955 Universal movie, the second in the series*
Right. *Jeff Morrow, Rex Reason and assembled scientists look over the lethal amphibian in* The Creature Walks Among Us *(Universal 1956)*

Again there was a lull, with no notable movies on the theme of Beauty and the Beast until Warner Brothers, cashing in on the short-lived boom for 3-D movies, had director Andre de Toth rapidly remake *The Mystery of The Wax Museum* as *House of Wax*, with Phyllis Kirk showing nothing of the lung power of Fay Wray, but Vincent Price as velvet-voiced and menacing as ever in the Lionel Atwill part. Among those present, and still credited in his real name, Charles Buchinski, was the future Charles Bronson. Audiences had chorus girls' legs,

flames and boiling wax thrust into their faces, and all this from a director who, because he had lost an eye, was entirely unable to see in depth or to view *House of Wax* in its intended three dimensions. Nonetheless, Technicolor melting wax figures in the blazing waxworks were unsettlingly queasy.

In 1954, Veronica Hurst was so besotted by her

love for Richard Carlson that, despite his protests and some very sinister asides from white-haired butler Michael Pate, she stayed on in his sinister Scottish castle, only to meet with the giant frog that was his 200-year-old ancestor in William Cameron Menzies' 3-D movie, *The Maze*. Despite what seemed like an insuperable genetic barrier to their future, love triumphs when the giant frog, terrified after meeting Miss Hurst in the Maze (she merely fainted!) hops back into his castle and, ignoring Michael Pate's soothing words, jumps to his death from a window. Miss Hurst and Mr Carlson (presumably) lived happily ever after!

Richard Carlson was also at hand in 1954 to witness with horror the abortive romance between Universal's latest monster, *The Creature From The Black Lagoon* and his abducted inamorata, Julia Adams. Jack Arnold not only directed the first movie of the Gill Man with considerable chilling effect, but also devised the Gill Man–after staring at an Academy Award in his office, he had come upon the idea of the basic "Oscar" body with gills and fins attached! His equally good sequel, 1955's *Revenge of The Creature* was set in Florida instead of the lagoon on the river Amazon. This time Lori Nelson was the object of his thwarted passions, and John Agar the hero, but after having her to

himself for a little while, the Creature sank into the water amidst whining bullets.

Anthony Quinn made a try for, and missed completely, the mantles of Chaney and Laughton in Jean Delannoy's *Notre Dame de Paris (The Hunchback of Notre Dame)* in 1956. Quinn managed to look neither monstrous nor lovable, and the film's only compensations came from the delectable sight of Gina Lollobrigida as Esmeralda. The ultimate in massive love for the human female was practised by 1957's *Womaneater*, a carnivorous plant from the Amazon kept in his laboratory by mad scientist George Coulouris and fed on its favourite diet–young women! Traditional flames quenched both the insatiable lover and its scientific guardian!

Surgical love for the daughter whose scarred face he was responsible for brought on the horror in Pierre Brasseur's performance in George Franju's *Les Yeux Sans Visage (Eyes Without a Face)* made in 1959. He brought a clinical probing to the story of unsuccessful transplants to Edith Scob's scarred face. A scene to churn even the strongest stomachs is his unflinching camera stare (with photography hauntingly carried out in monochrome by Eugene Shuftan) at a scene where the skin is carefully peeled away and lifted off the girl's face!

Roddy McDowall gets ready to start The Clay Man stomping again in It *(Goldstar 1966), with Allan Sellars as The Golem*

Peter Cushing, as Arthur Grimsdyke, rises from his grave to tear out Robin Phillips' heart in the Amicus/Metromedia movie Tales From The Crypt *made in 1971*

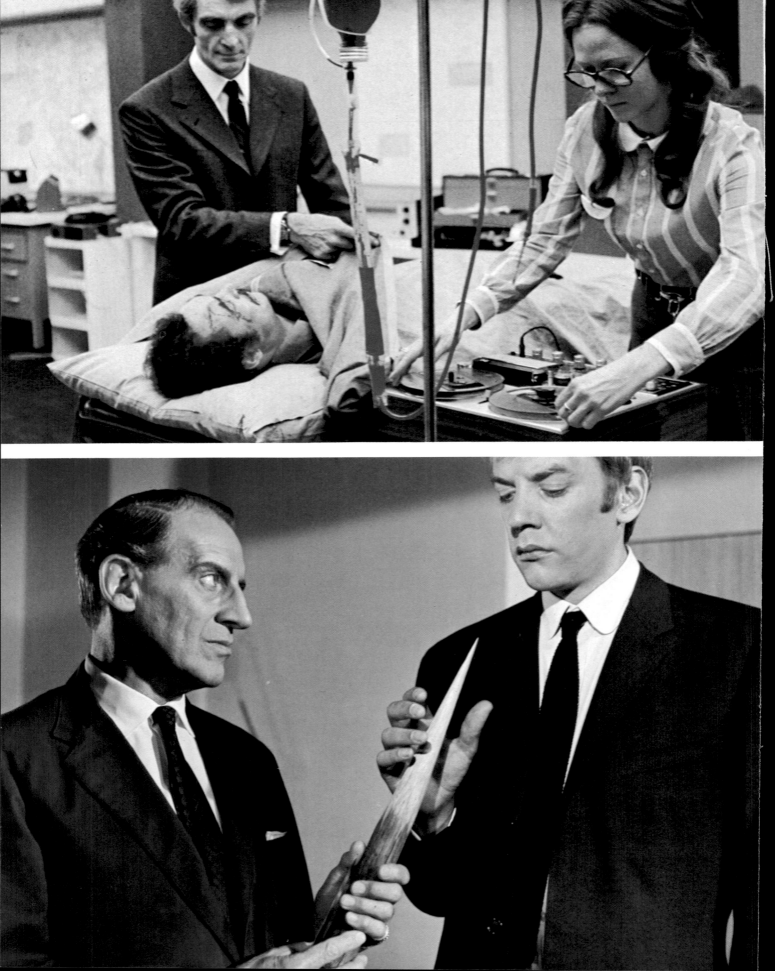

Lou Costello finally got a real dose of his own medicine when, in a solo movie, he married Dorothy Provine, *The Thirty Foot Bride of Candy Rock* (1959).

Terence Fisher added another classic to his portfolio when he made Hammer's colour version of *The Phantom of The Opera* in 1962. This time Herbert Lom was the scarred composer loose in the Paris catacombs, Heather Sears his unwilling singing pupil, and Thorley Walters supplied first rate comic relief in his role as the theatre manager.

King Kong made a surprising reappearance in 1963 in Japan, set to battle with Toho Studios reigning giant monster, Godzilla, in Inishiro Honda's *King Kong Tai Godzilla (King Kong Versus Godzilla)*, but his Oriental reincarnation, fighting Godzilla's radioactive halitosis, and operated, not by O'Brien's classic animation but by a wily Japanese gentleman inside his body, hardly seemed worth the effort. Only the climactic earthquake provided by special effects man Eiji Tsuburaya was respectably exciting.

In 1964, the Japanese *Kwaidan* illustrated the most corrupting end that unrequited love could bring. A young Samurai warrior divorces his wife so that he can marry again, this time for money. Returning to his first wife, he spends a night of love-making with her only to wake up the next morning to find her dead and decayed, a corpse beside him. The restrained direction and strangely ritualistic acting made *Kwaidan* noteworthy.

Monster-maker Ray Harryhausen provided a pterodactyl that presumably seized the very delectable Raquel Welch and carried her off in Hammer's spectacular remake of the Hal Roach-D. W. Griffith 1940 story of monsters and grunting prehistoric love, *One Million Years B.C.* Just for good measure, Harryhausen also provided battling giant reptiles and an enormous beach turtle. In 1967's *King Kong No Gyakushu (King Kong Escapes)* Rhodes Reason was the American presence in the movie and King Kong was discovered once more on his island home, this time battling with a dinosaur. Toho were sensible enough to introduce a love interest for Kong, in the shape of Linda Miller's Susan, hoisted into Kong's massive palm as though it was still 1933.

In 1969, in *The Oblong Box* Hilary Dwyer finds

Left. *Monstrous Marriage! Lou Costello weds Dorothy Provine, his* Thirty Foot Bride of Candy Rock *(DRB Productions 1959)*
Below. *Cavemen led by John Richardson prepare to attack with a giant reptile in Hammer's 1966* One Million Years B.C.

her love badly under strain when she goes to call her husband Julian (Vincent Price) for dinner, only to find him changing into a monster before her eyes, after being bitten in the hand by his brother, the cursed Alastair Williamson!

Motivated by love of his dead wife, Vincent Price as the horribly disfigured Dr Phibes sets out to murder all the medical men responsible for her death on the operating table in 1972's *The Abominable Dr Phibes*. Not content with mere killing for

his love's sake, the monstrous Dr Phibes, feeding himself delicately through a hole in the side of his neck and talking through an electric voice-trumpet, brings death to his victims in the shape of re-enactments of the plagues of the Bible! The first

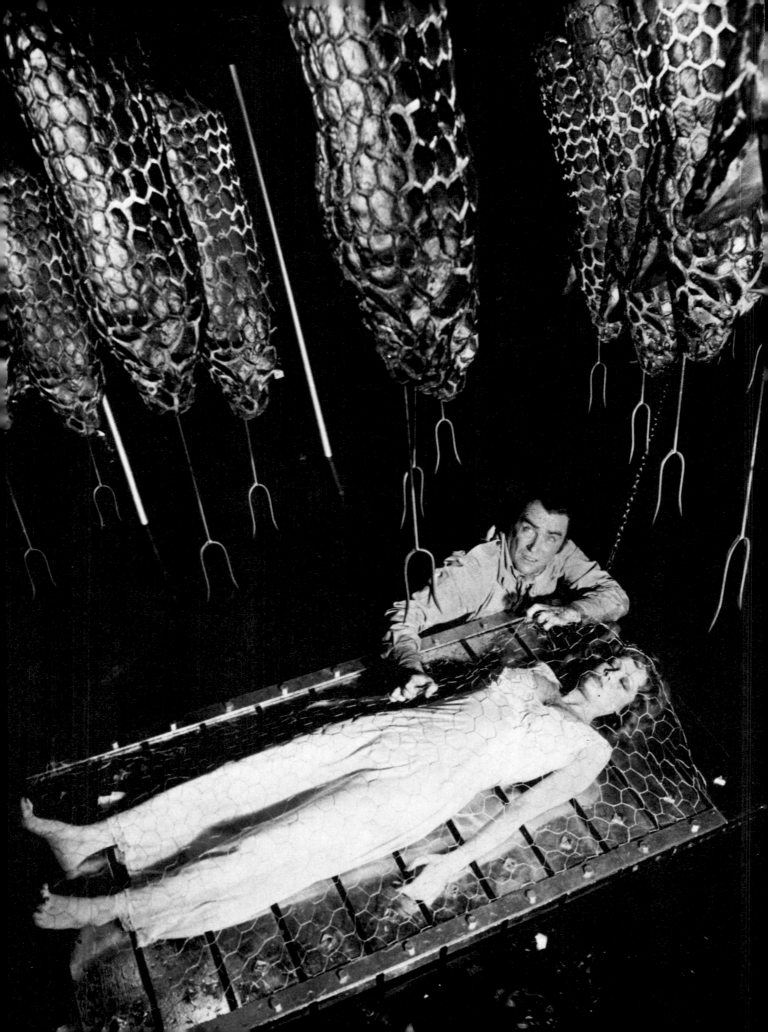

victim succumbs to bee stings, in mimicry of the curse of boils, and only after the second victim is killed by bats do the police, led by Peter Jeffrey's Inspector Trout, get on the trail of Price and his attractive assistant Vulnavia (Virginia North). But Price, director Robert Fuest and the audience have an immense amount of pleasure until, with one plague, that of darkness, still left unfinished, Price fills his body with preserving fluid and joins his dead but undecayed wife in their sealed vault for two!

Finally, there was a return to *The Phantom of The Opera* with 1974's rock opera version of the classic, *Phantom of The Paradise*. Director Brian de Palma adapted Leroux's tale and in bringing it up to date, went far beyond the point of parody. Jessica Harper provided the Beauty for William Finley's Beast. This time Finley's Phantom wears a golden mask to hide his deformities, caused when his face was smashed in a record press. Other, even more glaring incongruities abound, not least the deafening music echoing around the Rock Palace that has replaced the Opera House. Certainly, the manifestations of monstrous love that are to come will be not only better than *The Phantom of The Paradise*, but, hopefully, considerably less noisy!

Above. *Peter Cushing, as Dr. Lawrence, gives a beautifully judged performance of gothic menace in Freddie Francis'* The Ghoul *(Tyburn 1975).* Below. The Ghoul, *Don Henderson, advances on Alexandra Bastedo in another scene from the movie (Photographs courtesy Tyburn Film Productions)*

Above. *Larry 'Buster' Crabbe, Universal serial stalwart finds himself in a typical 'To Be Continued' situation*
Below. *Enclosed in ice,* The Thing *(RKO 1951) awaits thawing in the Arctic military base in Christian Nyby's classic movie*
Right. *Armed alien. One of William Cameron Manzies'* Invaders From Mars *(20th Century-Fox 1953), complete with mandatory ray-gun*

NOTHER WORLD

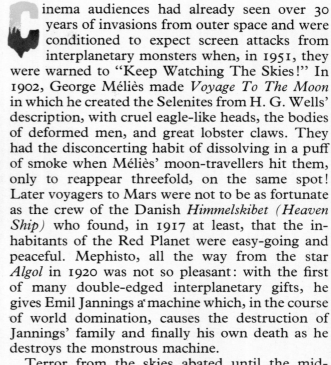

Cinema audiences had already seen over 30 years of invasions from outer space and were conditioned to expect screen attacks from interplanetary monsters when, in 1951, they were warned to "Keep Watching The Skies!" In 1902, George Méliès made *Voyage To The Moon* in which he created the Selenites from H. G. Wells' description, with cruel eagle-like heads, the bodies of deformed men, and great lobster claws. They had the disconcerting habit of dissolving in a puff of smoke when Méliès' moon-travellers hit them, only to reappear threefold, on the same spot! Later voyagers to Mars were not to be as fortunate as the crew of the Danish *Himmelskibet (Heaven Ship)* who found, in 1917 at least, that the inhabitants of the Red Planet were easy-going and peaceful. Mephisto, all the way from the star *Algol* in 1920 was not so pleasant: with the first of many double-edged interplanetary gifts, he gives Emil Jannings a machine which, in the course of world domination, causes the destruction of Jannings' family and finally his own death as he destroys the monstrous machine.

Terror from the skies abated until the mid-Thirties when Universal made their tatty but immensely fascinating serials of the comic-strip hero, Flash Gordon. Buster Crabbe, his hair died blond for the part, was Gordon, in 1936's *Flash Gordon*, 1938's *Flash Gordon's Trip to Mars* and 1940's *Flash Gordon Conquers The Universe*. In all three, he was busy saving the Earth from enslavement by evil tyrant Ming The Merciless, ruler of the planet of Mongo. By careful use of sets left standing from other, more prestigious movies, Universal set a standard for the fantasy-horror serials that was to last their relatively short span of popularity.

1950 was the prelude to the main years of space monsters with one of the last serials, from Republic Studios, which had Walter Reed as *The Flying Disc Man From Mars* (Mars was still the favourite invading planet, its canals having not yet been disproved). "B" feature terror came to Denver Pyle and others in the same year's *The Flying Saucer* which made its attack in one of the genre's most popular landing sites, Alaska. *Rocket Ship X-M* was made fast by director Kurt Neumann to cash in on the popularity of George Pal's *Destination Moon* in 1950, actually beating it into the cinema, and exposing crew members Lloyd Bridges and Hugh O'Brian to a fusilade of hostile rocks from the unfriendly natives of Mars!

Left. *Richard Carlson advances on the alien space vessel in* It Came From Outer Space *(Universal 1953)*
Opposite top. *Patricia Laffan as the* Devil Girl From Mars *(Danzigers 1954), seen here in front of a studio back-drop*
Opposite bottom. *Another Ray Harryhausen creation, the Rhedosaurus, tramples New York in Eugene Lourie's* The Beast From 20,000 Fathoms *(WB 1953)*

But 1951 was the year in which Earth really settled down to enjoy extra-terrestrial horror. Lesley Selander directed Cameron Mitchell and Arthur Franz in *Flight To Mars*, where Mitchell found that all space travel wasn't tough when he met up with shapely Martian Alita in the form of Marguerite Chapman, and Edgar G. Ulmer made *The Man From Planet X*. This unpleasant-looking creation, with his high-domed poker face under its glass helmet, landed in a hollywood fog on a remote Scottish island, there to spread terror among the locals. Like many monsters to follow, he perished at the hands of the army, in this case the British with anti-tank guns. One of the largest interplanetary monsters, responsible for the death of the planet Earth, except for a space-ship full of chosen survivors, was the star Bellus which hit the Earth in George Pal's *When Worlds Collide* in 1951. Rudolph Mate, Dreyer's cinematographer on *Vampyr*, directed nominal stars Richard Derr and Barbara Rush, but the real star was Paramount Studios, whose terrifying special effects of the end of the world won for the movie an Academy Award. However, it was visitors from outer space James Arness in *The Thing* and Michael Rennie and his nine-foot robot Gort who were to make a landmark of the genre.

The Thing was tautly scripted by Charles Lederer from John W. Campbell Jr's story *Who Goes There?* and was directed at a cracking pace by Christian Nyby. The Thing is found under the Arctic ice in a crashed flying saucer, and is all that remains when over-keen Keith Tobey, trying to thaw out the monster craft, destroys it with a thermite bomb. Still in its block of ice, The Thing, the body of the saucer's crewman, is taken back to an air force base by Tobey, there to be accidentally thawed out by an electric blanket unwittingly left over the ice. Alive again, The Thing is soon cutting a swathe of terror through the base, murdering airmen and scientists and dogs, one of which tears off an arm. Soon the arm is growing apace in the form of little, nasty "plants", fed on plasma.

A stunned Douglas Spencer announces it as "an intellectual carrot! The mind boggles". Tobey makes up for his carelessness by destroying it, following the inspired suggestion of Margaret Sheridan who says: "What do you do with a vegetable? You cook it!" Which is just what Tobey does, making an electric booby-trap which incinerates the monster in one of the movie's most powerful scenes. The Thing, screaming as it burns, was 6 ft. 5 in. James Arness, making his screen debut and soon to find stardom on television as Matt Dillon.

Also in 1951, a 350-foot Flying Saucer brought Michael Rennie as Klaatu to the grounds of the White House in *The Day The Earth Stood Still*. Rennie had come to warn the world to discontinue their tests of atomic weapons or suffer total destruction at the hands of extra-terrestrial powers. With him is his robot, Gort, who is programmed to carry out the death sentence on the planet. To prove that his is no idle threat, Klaatu brings the Earth to a standstill by neutralizing all electrical power on the planet, with the humane exceptions of hospitals and aircraft in flight. Fortunately for a short-sighted world, Klaatu finds an understanding of human love and emotions in his friendship with a widow (Patricia Neal) and her son (Billy Gray). Patricia Neal is able to stop Gort from destroying the world after Klaatu has been killed by an unbelieving group of Earthmen as he returns to his Flying Saucer.

1952 was far from a vintage year: memorable only as the last credited screenplay from the co-writer of *Dracula* and *Frankenstein*, John L. Balderston, the terrible *Red Planet Mars* has Peter Graves in touch with the 300-year-old inhabitants of the Red Planet. Like so many other movie scientists, Graves is forced to blow himself, his wife and the villain to pieces, but not before Communism has been wiped from the face of the Soviet Union!

1953 had the 3-D multi-armed green Martian, sinisterly floating in a transparent globe and taking over people's bodies and minds by the budget-saving process of inserting crystals into their brains! Made by William Cameron Menzies, *Invaders from Mars* showed signs of a tight budget but as the young boy who sees the invaders land in the flying saucer and then take over the minds of his parents, Jimmy Hunt was convincing, particularly in some well-played scenes with Arthur Franz as a helpful scientist.

W. Lee Wilder, brother of the more famous Billy, made 1953's *Phantom From Space*. This

monster lands in California and after killing two people and scrambling local radar (a favourite ploy of extra-terrestrial monsters) it turns out to be an invisible creature able to survive only in its space suit. Unable to breathe without its own atmosphere, the Phantom appears briefly as a bald-domed, muscle-bound American football player, before disintegrating in front of his pursuers!

George Pal ensured 1953's place in the history of movie monsterdom with *War of The Worlds* in which he transposed the action from southern England, as envisaged by H. G. Wells, to California. The basic premise of the story remained unchanged, however, and Byron Haskin directed with a visual flair that served the battles between the Earthmen and the Martians well, if turning nominal hero and heroine Gene Barry and Ann Robinson into ciphers. The movie is full of fine sequences: the landing of the rocket ships, the appearance of the manta-ray-like flying vehicles with their probing eyes on flexible stalks and their searing death rays, the one appearance of an actual "Martian", in a sequence in which the suspense is sedulously built up as Barry and Robinson are tracked in a deserted farmhouse destroyed by the impact of a crashing spaceship. The Martian was not a let-down, as many space monsters are, because director Haskin wisely allowed audiences only a fleeting glimpse of the single-eyed, sucker-fingered horror.

Below. *The end of a hunt. Scientists discover the giant ants' nest deep in the Los Angeles storm drain in the 1953 Warner Bros movie* Them! *Right. Serial strong man. Judd Holden as a ray-gun-packing hero from Columbia's 1953* The Lost Planet

Below. Satan's Satellites, *a 70-minute feature film version of the 1952 Republic serial* Zombies of The Stratosphere Bottom. *Paul Campbell and Craig Stevens find a piece of the giant insect in* The Deadly Mantis *(Universal 1957)*

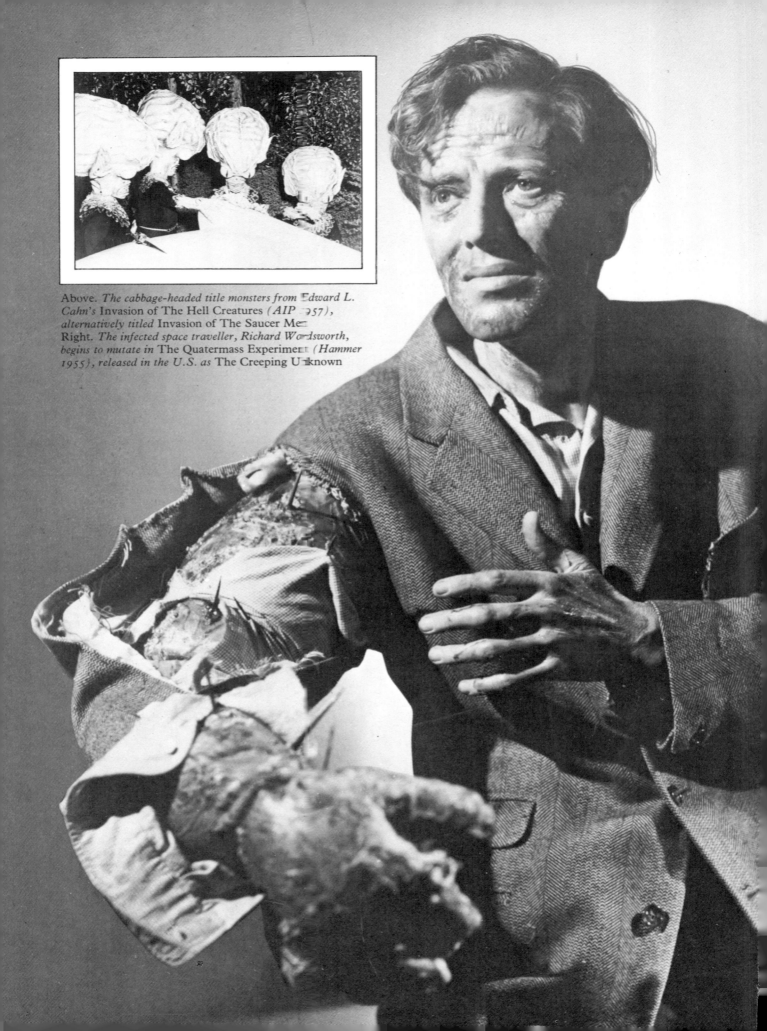

Above. *The cabbage-headed title monsters from* Edward L. Cahn's Invasion of The Hell Creatures *(AIP 1957), alternatively titled* Invasion of The Saucer Men. Right. *The infected space traveller, Richard Wordsworth, begins to mutate in* The Quatermass Experiment *(Hammer 1955), released in the U.S. as* The Creeping Unknown

The movie's real stars were the Paramount special effects team who supervised the terrifying scenes of the destruction of Los Angeles by the Martians' flying machines and the searing incineration of humans foolhardy enough to go against their death rays. The Martians proved immune to all that the puny humans could bring against them, even shrugging off the atomic bomb under their protective shields of pure force. Once more Paramount received an Academy Award for Special Effects.

The other key movie in the genre was 1953's *It Came From Outer Space*, a masterpiece that retains its power even when shown "flat" and not in its original 3-D. From Ray Bradbury's story, Harry Essex wrote a deceptively simple screenplay and Jack Arnold directed the whole without putting one frame wrong. Set in the Arizona desert, *It Came From Outer Space* follows amateur astronomer John Putnam, played by Richard Carlson, as he tries to convince the local powers that a spaceship has landed and buried itself in the desert. Capable of assuming the forms of all sorts of life, the occupants of the spacecraft take over the bodies of local inhabitants, including Putnam's sweetheart (Barbara Rush). Finally managing to convince the townspeople that visitors from Outer Space have landed, Putnam discovers from the aliens that they are only grounded on Earth for as long as it takes for them to effect necessary repairs to their spacecraft. From this relatively simple story line, Jack Arnold made *It Came From Outer Space* into a classic movie and arguably one which used the 3-D process to best effect.

1955 saw Hammer enter the outer space monster genre with their movie version of Nigel Kneale's gripping television serial *The Quatermass Xperiment*, which had kept Britons enslaved in front of their

Below left. Rex Reason is attacked by the Metalunan Mutant in Universal's special effects masterpiece This Island Earth, *directed by Joseph Newman in 1955. Below right. Ray 'Crash' Corrigan makes a repulsive Monster in his title performance as* It, The Terror From Beyond Space *(UA 1958)*

Left. Dana Wynter, King Donovan, Carolyn Jones and Kevin McCarthy advance on the growing pods in Don Siegel's Invasion of The Body Snatchers *(Allied Artists 1956)*
Bottom left. Professor Quatermass, Brian Donlevy, surveys the stigma of alien infection on Bryan Forbes' cheek in Quatermass II *(Hammer 1957)*

technological marvels ravaged by inter-stellar wars, was impressive. Edwin Parker, Universal's double for Lon Chaney Jr's Wolf Man and Frankenstein monster, took to Technicolor this time as the Mutant, with huge exposed brain, insect-like carapace, bulging eyes and lobster's claws.

In David Kramarsky's *The Beast With A Million Eyes*, producer Roger Corman invaded the same Arizona desert as had Jack Arnold with *It Came From Outer Space*. This cold little film has the aliens taking over the minds of animals and turning them terrifyingly against man. Once more the invaders from Outer Space are invisible but scenes of a cow being possessed by the aliens, to turn and savage its owner, have power above the general appearance of the film and some poor acting.

television sets through 1953. The film broke into the American market for Hammer Films, where United Artists entitled it *The Creeping Unknown* and Val Guest made a fine job of directing Richard Wordsworth as the infected survivor of a British space probe, mutating tragically into a hideous monster as he drags his painful way across London. Brian Donlevy plays the eponymous Professor Quatermass who finally arranges the monster's death by electrocution when it is cornered in Westminster Abbey. Its range of brilliant special effects which, among other delights, created the world of Metaluna with its futuristic cities and

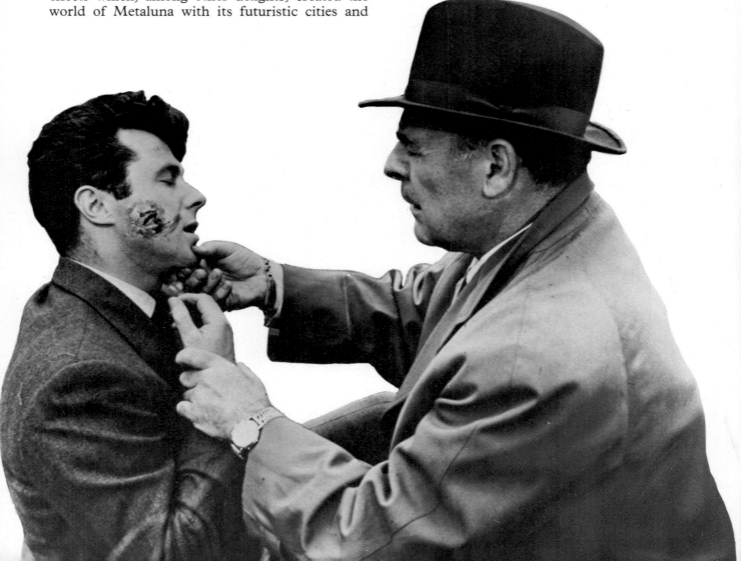

Metro-Goldwyn-Mayer turned to Walt Disney's animators to provide the terrible roaring lion-like Monster of The Id which attacks members of the crew of United Planets Starship C57D when it makes its base on the *Forbidden Planet*. The Monster turns out to be the evil projection of the planet's owner, Morbius (Walter Pidgeon), channelling the incredible energy sources of the Krel, the now-dead previous inhabitants of Altair IV. The movie, engagingly acted by Pidgeon, Leslie Nielsen, as the Commander of the spaceship, and Earl Holliman, with Robby the Robot as the film's comic relief, was an ingenious re-working of Shakespeare's *The Tempest*. On a less elevated level, Hammer continued extra-terrestrial horror with the giant creeping semolina in 1956's *X the Unknown*. This was Jimmy Sangster's first script, a sequel to the successful *Quatermass Xperiment*.

Don Siegel in 1956 made the extremely terrifying and deceptively simple *The Invasion of The Body Snatchers*. Behind the catchpenny title is a film which superbly evokes the very real horror of the monster of the soul, the terror that can assume human form but make that human form infinitely more frightening than anything that is merely human. Siegel was well served by his cast, notably Kevin McCarthy and Dana Wynter as the leads, and King Donovan and Carolyn Jones in support, and by the screenplay of Daniel Mainwaring. McCarthy played Dr Miles Bennell who returns to his home town of Santa Mira only to find it in the grip of what he at first believes is an attack of mass hysteria, as children claim their parents are "changed" in some terrible way, and families are split into those who have "changed" and those who just know that something is terribly wrong.

Dr Bennell is called to the home of Jack (King Donovan) and Theodora (Carolyn Jones) to find, incongruously displayed on the baize of a billiard table, a waxen likeness of Jack, a corpse that is alive and growing progressively more like Jack. Later Miles finds giant seedpods in his own cellar,

growing obscenely under bubbling foam into
simulacra of himself and his fiancee Becky (Dana
Wynter). These "pods", the "fruit" of seeds
which have drifted down to Earth from space, are
the body snatchers, pseudo-human organisms
which take over the minds of humans as they sleep,
to leave them totally without feelings, the perfect
zombies. Miles and Becky flee to the sheriff for
help, only to find him, like the rest of the townspeople, translated into an other-world being. He
tries to persuade them to join the Undead.

Miles and Becky manage to escape to his surgery,
there to fight desperately with the aid of drugs
against the sleep that will rob them of their souls.
Visited next morning by his fellow doctor, Daniel
Kaufman (Larry Gates), and Jack, both now taken
over, Miles manages to avoid their blandishments
to ". . . be reborn into a new body that will never
feel pain again", and escapes with Becky from the
terrifying pursuit of the town's whole population,
deflected from their task of loading the pods onto
trucks to take the infection to new cities. Finding
temporary shelter in a mine shaft high above the
town, Miles leaves Becky for a moment. When he
returns he finds she has fallen asleep and been taken
over—a moment of pure horror as Miles recoils
from her dead embrace.

The film should have ended on a scene of
hopeless terror as Miles ran unheeded among the
speeding traffic of a freeway, crying out to the

passing motorists, "You're next! You're next!",
but Allied Artists forced Siegel to frame the whole
story in a flashback format: Miles tells an unbelieving Whit Bissell of the events in Santa Mira,
to be proven at the end as a truck is rammed,
disgorging its deadly load of pods. But even this
enforced ending could not take away from the
powerful tension generated by the movie, particularly in those scenes where McCarthy suffered
the persuasion of the Undead to become one of
them.

The rest of the movies of 1956 were routine:
Roger Corman had Paul Blaisdell as a giant extra-
terrestrial with a disconcerting habit of firing
missiles into the cast's skulls in *It Conquered The
World*, and Bela Lugosi appeared as The Ghoul
Man in Edward D. Wood Junior's *Plan Nine
From Outer Space*, a ludicrous movie with television's Vampira. The parts were barely fleshed out
in a farrago of bodies brought back to life from the
influence of visitors from Outer Space It was
tragic that this should have been Lugosi's last film,
since a more unfitting epitaph would have been
hard to devise.

1957 was the year that real life caught up with
monster movies, when the Russians launched
Sputnik. In the cinema, however, an American
rocket ship crashed off the coast of Sicily on its
return from Venus, to provide a splendid movie
monster, the Ymir, animated by master creator of

impossible creatures, Ray Harryhausen, in Nathan Juran's *Twenty Million Miles to Earth*. The Ymir hatches from an egg brought back from Venus and grows into a giant scaly creature over 20 feet in height, which terrorizes the Italian countryside before meeting its nemesis, as ever at the hands of the army, in the ruins of the Roman Coliseum.

The Monolith Monsters, based on a story by Jack Arnold and directed with verve by John Sherwood, had humans turning to stone by contact with an element from Outer Space which thrives on water. The stabbing crystals of the monolith monsters themselves, decimating the desert community, added to the range of Universal monsters. Malformed green creatures, with huge veined heads like giant cabbages, nasty bulging eyes and needles that sprang from their fingers were invaders from Mars in *Invasion of The Saucermen*, a bad attack of the "B" feature creatures. Paul Birch in sunglasses and an inscrutable expression looked the world over as a possible invasion site in Roger Corman's *Not of This Earth*. Extra-terrestrial beings descended on England and caused fungus growths to sprout from the faces of their victims, including Bryan Forbes, in Hammer's *Quatermass II*, until Brian Donlevy, once more playing the Professor, destroys them. *Kronos* provided a unique monster from the skies: it lands on a California beach and becomes a towering marching machine that stamps its way across the countryside, finally killing itself with indigestion as it drains the power from one electrical generating station too many!

The following year saw the beginning of a decline in the genre. However, an exception was made with *I Married a Monster From Outer Space*, a movie that was considerably better than its title. Tom Tryon is "taken over" by aliens as he watches their space vessel land. Unfortunately, the next day sees him married to Gloria Talbot, and, needless to say, she does not enjoy her honeymoon!

Forrest Tucker battled with giant spiders and caterpillars in the British *The Strange World of Planet X*, but a promising idea was made less effective by poor special effects which showed only too clearly that the giant insects were inserted close-ups of the real things.

Although *The Astonishing She-Monster* turned out to be a bearer of good tidings from the Galaxy to Earth, it did not prevent this female horror from being able to kill, not just with the touch of her radioactive body, but also, literally, to slay with a glance! Richard Devon was the next in a long line of Earthmen to be taken over by extra-terrestrial beings in *War of The Satellites*, but, although adding a pleasantly gaunt presence to the movie, he failed to sabotage the United Nations rocket programme!

1959 saw a continuation of the decline of interplanetary monsters. *The Teenagers from Outer Space* brought with them the Gargon terror, but it

turned out to be a much magnified and somewhat placid lobster. *The Cosmic Man* was John Carradine, a visitor to this planet who has to prove his ultimate goodwill by curing crippled Scotty Morrow who is able to walk again in the last reel. Arthur Franz as Commander Holloway guided *The Atomic Submarine* under the ice to find yet another Flying Saucer at the North Pole, with its tentacled occupants getting ready to take over the Earth. They are foiled by the intrepid Holloway who converts one of his submarine's torpedoes into an air missile which shoots down the Saucer as it takes off! Japan's Inishiro Honda and Toho's brilliant special effects man, Eiji Tsuburaya, joined the act with *Uchu Dai Senso (Battle in Outer Space)* which sees Earth menaced by an interplanetary army marshalled on the Moon, before the invaders are despatched in the vivid title battle.

In 1960, the Universe sent one of its least pleasant invaders with Jerry Lewis as Kreton in the movie version of Gore Vidal's *Visitor To A Small Planet*, and continued its terrifying assault on Earth with the incubated unEarthly children in Wolf Rilla's *Village of The Damned*. This was an intelligent adaptation of John Wyndham's chilling novel, *The Midwich Cuckoos* (far superior to the 1963 effort, *Children of the Damned*), and, despite a low budget, Rilla extracted every ounce of terror from the story of the murderous children born in a village where all the women had been made pregnant by some strange out-of-this-world influence. Particularly effective is the scene as four of the children, led by the astoundingly evil-looking Martin Stephens, form a living pattern and force, through the power of their minds, Thomas Heathcot to turn his shotgun from them and direct its fire into his own mouth instead.

Improbably Howard Keel starred in 1962's *The Day of The Triffids*, giant, mobile and death-dealing plants brought to life though a rain of

Far left. The H-Man (*Toho 1958*). Left. *Peter Cushing, Roberta Tovey and Jennie Linden* in Dr Who And The Daleks (*Aaru 1965*). Below left. Mothra (*Toho 1961*)
Below right. *Charlton Heston in* Planet of The Apes (*20th Century-Fox 1968*). Right. *Andrew Keir in* Quatermass And The Pit (*Hammer 1967*)

meteorites that blinded most of the world. Director
Steve Sekely extracted as much horror as he could
from the situation, and the plants themselves
proved pleasingly horrific, giving stung victim
Mervyn Johns a gruesome green pallor in death!

Only a part of the astronaut returning from the
moon and screaming "Kill! It makes me kill, kill!"
provided the monster in *The Crawling Hand*
directed by Herbert L. Strock in 1963. The hand
was all that was left of the unfortunate space
traveller, but it made up for its lack of stature with
some fine evil, twitching compulsively and strangl-
ing Mrs Hotchkiss, before being destroyed by a
pack of starving wild-cats! Gabriella Licudi was the
Unearthly Stranger in John Krish's fine low-
budget movie. The advance guard for invading
women from another galaxy, she deals out death in
a malevolent way, only softening in her love for her
husband John Neville, and disturbingly scarring
her face with burned furrows when she lets herself
cry.

1964 saw Lionel Jeffries and Edward Judd,
along with decorative Martha Hyer, face Ray
Harryhausen's Technicolor moon-monsters in
Nathan Juran's *First Men In The Moon*. The
creatures were good, notably a giant caterpillar,

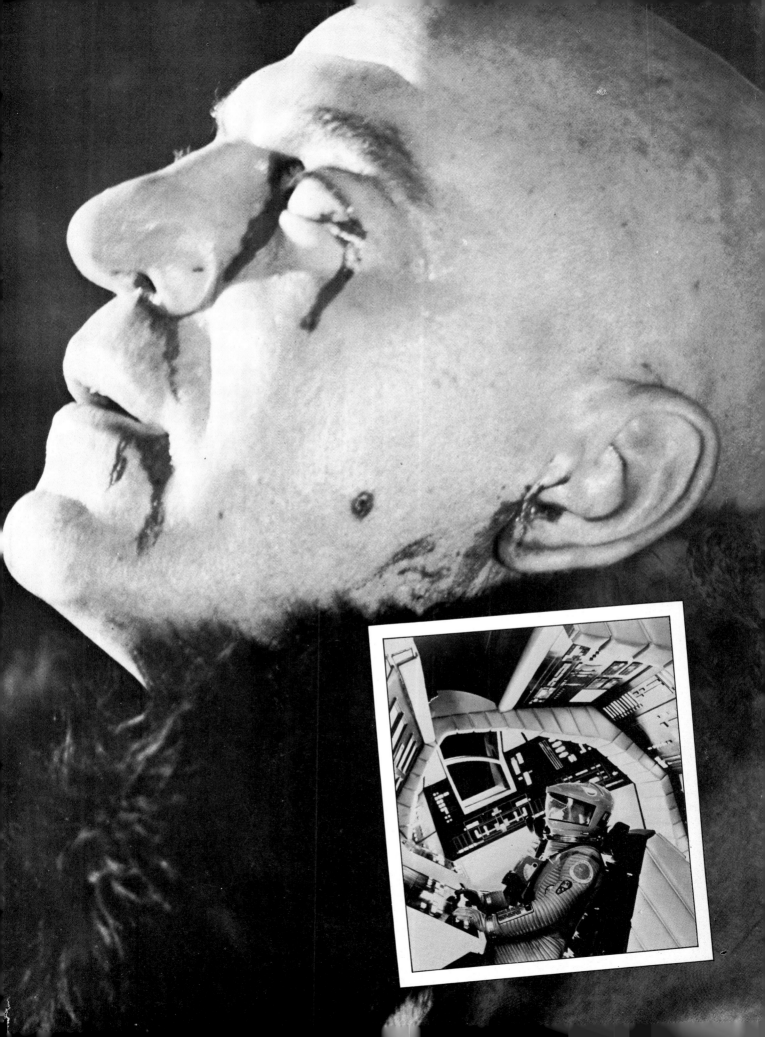

and the Selenites suddenly hibernating in crisp cobweb cocoons during an eclipse would have pleased H. G. Wells himself. *Robinson Crusoe on Mars* was astronaut Paul Mantee crashed on the Red Planet and under attack from some particularly nasty interplanetary creatures in Byron Haskin's movie. The film was shot, in fact, in California's Death Valley, and the bleak savagery of that landscape stood in eerily for the Martian terrain.

In 1965, Boris Karloff as Nahum Whitley created strange organisms under the influence of rays from a meteorite buried in his Arkham cellar, before himself becoming a monster under the influence of the visitor from space in *Die, Monster, Die*. Roger Corman's one-time art director, Daniel Haller directed the colour version of H. P. Lovecraft's *The Colour Out of Space* with some of his mentor's flair, and his creation of the greenhouse with its luxuriant radiation-changed plants was particularly unsettling. Karloff was as good as ever, both as the sinister Nahum and as the monster, throbbing with strange light that the radiating meteor had created.

The Daleks, bizarre metallic robots with mechanical humming voices and probably the most popular stars ever created by the BBC, came to the big screen in *Dr Who and The Daleks* in the same year. Peter Cushing was their nemesis. The metal monsters were sufficiently popular to make a reappearance the following year, 1966, in Gordon Flemyng's *Daleks – Invasion Earth 2150 A.D.*, again pursued by Peter Cushing's delightful Dr Who, this time destroying the monsters by means of a powerful magnetic force which he released against them.

Quatermass, this time incarnated in the form of Andrew Keir, returned in the first colour film of the series in 1967, Hammer's *Quatermass and The Pit*. The movie provides a nice line in monsters with giant green locusts from Mars, and a final climactic appearance of the Martian terror in the form of a giant devil over London, destroyed when Professor Quatermass propels a huge crane into it.

Planet of The Apes, directed by Franklin Schaffner, was by far the most intelligent of the series, with Charlton Heston as an astronaut flung into a nightmare future where man is the slave and the world, an Earth shown in the last sequence to be the result of an atomic holocaust, ruled by intelligent apes. The make-up devised by Twentieth Century-Fox for their simian monsters was as effective as anything to come out of the heyday of Jack Pierce at Universal, and Roddy McDowall, Kim Hunter and Maurice Evans were able to add their touches of character to make the apes paradoxically both more human and more terrifyingly bestial.

Terence Fisher deployed Peter Cushing and Christopher Lee in the fight against interplanetary invaders which burned islanders alive in 1967's *Night of The Big Heat*. These invaders look unstoppable until the *deus ex machina* of a thunderstorm destroys the creatures without intervention from Man. Freddie Francis took the helm for Amicus *They Came From Beyond Space*, an adaptation by Milton Subotsky of Joseph Millard's *The Gods Hate Kansas*, with the locale changed from America to Cornwall. Here Robert Hutton, as Dr Curtis Temple, finds that extra-terrestrial beings are behind the outbreak of a mysterious plague decimating the countryside.

1968 was the year Stanley Kubrick created a computer monster with Hal, in his gadget-obsessed film, *2001 – A Space Odyssey*. Apart from the meticulous special effects by Wally Veevers, Douglas Trumbull, Con Pederson and Tom Howard, with a sequence through the "Time Warping Star Gate" the film was overlong. It also lacked any human interest, apart from the sardonic character of Hal, beautifully voiced by actor Douglas Rain. The movie roared to box-office and cult success, not a little helped by American college students who saw in Kubrick's confused ending an echo of the prevalent drug culture, so that *2001* became, for audiences and publicists alike, "The Ultimate Trip".

The Body Stealers came from space in 1969 to snatch parachutists in mid-air in an enveloping red mist, and then keep their bodies in suspended animation to repopulate their home planet. In Gerry Levy's sadly lethargic movie, the aliens also take over the body of Maurice Evans' Dr Matthews and cause considerable heart-searching in George Sanders and on the part of the inventor of a new parachute, Neil Connery.

1970 saw terror from outer space in the form of a lethal disease fought by the cast of Robert Wise's *The Andromeda Strain* and the last movie of note in the genre was *Son of The Blob*, in 1972, a pallid imitation of *The Blob*, which in 1958 had needed no less than the youthful Steve McQueen to destroy it with a fire extinguisher, a fitting death for a movie monster with the incredible gall to engulf and decimate a cinema!

158

We should like to thank the individuals and organisations who have helped us with the preparation of this book, particularly the National Film Archive, Gary Parfitt, Syndication International, and the numerous production companies mentioned in the captions.